Eternal Values

Living a Meaningful, Moral, and Inspired Life of Torah Values.

Based on the teachings and advice of our Sages, works of Chasidut and insights of the Lubavitcher Rebbe.

Translated from *Kuntres De'ot, Midot v'Hanhagot Tovot*, found in *Sefer Kitzur Halachot L'Avot Uvanim*

Compiled by Rabbi I. D. Silverman

ETERNAL VALUES

mail@eternal-values.com

Published by
KEHOT PUBLICATION SOCIETY
770 Eastern Parkway / Brooklyn, New York 11213
718-774-4000 • fax 718-774-2718
editor@kehot.com

ORDER DEPARTMENT:
291 Kingston Avenue / Brooklyn, New York 11213
718-778-0226 • fax 718-778-4148
www.kehot.com

ISBN 978-0-8266-0760-7

Printed in the United States of America

Preface

We are proud to present *Eternal Values—Living a Meaningful, Moral, and Inspired Life of Torah Values*, a work containing teachings and advice from our Sages on the proper values of life, correct outlook, good character, and upright behavior according to the Torah as befitting a person chosen to serve G-d, the Creator of the universe.

The work is primarily based on Rambam's *Hilchot De'ot*, various chapters of the *Tanya* and *Shulchan Aruch* by R. Schneur Zalman of Liadi, sections of the *Kitzur Shulchan Aruch*, works of Chasidut, and *Likkutei Sichot* by the Lubavitcher Rebbe, Rabbi Menachem M. Schneerson, of righteous memory.

Included within the text are numerous stories and examples of the conduct and customs of our great ancestors—Biblical figures, Talmudic Sages, righteous personalities, early Chasidim, and "men of great deeds"—throughout the ages. Their gift to us is the gift of their example—how one should think and behave.

The work was compiled and translated by Rabbi I. D. Silverman. Special thanks are due to Rabbi Avraham D. Vaisfiche for reviewing the text, to Rabbis Yosef B. Friedman and Rabbi Dovid Olidort for their editorial guidance, and to Rabbis Yirmi Berkowitz and Mendel Laine for coordinating the project.

Kehot Publication Society

18 Elul 5777

Contents

Introduction VII

PART ONE 1

Our Relationship with Hashem

1 אֱמוּנָה בַּה׳ 2

Belief in Hashem

2 ״שִׁוִּיתִי ה׳ לְנֶגְדִּי תָמִיד״ 7

"I have placed Hashem before me constantly"—To live with the constant mindfulness of being in Hashem's presence at all times

3 הַשְׁגָּחָה פְּרָטִית—
הָאֱמוּנָה בְּהַשְׁגָּחָה אֱלוֹקִית עַל הַכֹּל 11

Belief in Divine Providence

4 לִמּוּד הוֹרָאָה מִכָּל דָּבָר שֶׁרוֹאִים אוֹ שׁוֹמְעִים 15

To learn a life lesson from everything one sees or hears

5 ״אֵין רָע יוֹרֵד מִלְמַעְלָה״ –
שׁוּם דָּבָר שְׁלִילִי לֹא בָּא מֵאֵת ה׳ 19

No negativity descends from Heaven

6 לְבָרֵךְ עַל הָרָע כְּשֵׁם שֶׁמְּבָרְכִים עַל הַטּוֹב 23

The obligation to bless G-d for the "negative" as well as for the "positive"

7 בִּטָּחוֹן בַּה׳ 27

Trust in Hashem

8 אַל יֵאוּשׁ—לְעוֹלָם לֹא לְאַבֵּד אֶת הַתִּקְוָה 32

Never lose hope

9 מִדָּה כְּנֶגֶד מִדָּה—כָּךְ הִיא הַנְהָגַת
הַקָּדוֹשׁ בָּרוּךְ הוּא עִם הָאָדָם 35

Measure for measure

10 אֵין הַקָּבָּ״ה מְבַקֵּשׁ אֶלָּא לְפִי
כֹּחַ שֶׁל כָּל אֶחָד וְאֶחָד 37

G-d requests from each one only according to his ability

11 קִדּוּשׁ הַשֵּׁם—לְקַדֵּשׁ (וְלֹא לְחַלֵּל) שֵׁם שָׁמַיִם 41

Sanctification of Hashem's name—*"Kiddush Hashem"*

12 ״כָּל מַעֲשֶׂיךָ יִהְיוּ לְשֵׁם שָׁמַיִם״ 45

All of one's actions should be for the sake of Heaven

PART TWO 49

Our Relationship with Ourselves

13a שִׂמְחָה 50

Joy

13b שִׂמְחָה שֶׁל מִצְוָה—
שִׂמְחָה הַנּוֹבַעַת מִקִּיּוּם הַמִּצְווֹת 55

The joy derived from *mitzvot*

14 הַכָּרַת הַטּוֹב—
לְהוֹקִיר וּלְהַעֲרִיךְ מַעֲשִׂים טוֹבִים 58

Gratitude and acknowledging goodness

15a הִסְתַּפְּקוּת 63

Satisfaction (even with little)

15b שָׂמֵחַ בְּחֶלְקוֹ 67

Rejoicing in one's lot

16 זְרִיזוּת, הִתְלַהֲבוּת, וְאוֹמֶץ הַלֵּב בַּעֲבוֹדַת ה' 70
Energy, enthusiasm, and courage of heart in the service of Hashem

17 מוֹחַ שַׁלִּיט עַל הַלֵּב 75
The imperative that the head should rule the heart—"mind over matter"

18 לְכַתְחִלָּה אַרִיבֶּער—"לִחְיוֹת מֵעַל הַמִּכְשׁוֹלִים" 79
Living above obstacles (leaping "over" rather than going "under" an obstacle)

19 הַתְמָדָה 83
Persistence

20 מִדַּת הָאֱמֶת 86
Truthfulness

21 נֶאֱמָנוּת 92
Trustworthiness

22 קִיּוּם הַחְלָטוֹת 95
Fulfilling personal resolutions

23 מַעֲבִיר עַל מִדּוֹתָיו
—הִתְגַּבְּרוּת עַל הַדַּחַף לִנְקוֹם 98
Overcoming the desire for retribution

24 הִתְרַחֲקוּת מֵהַכַּעַס 100
Keeping away from anger

25 נְדִיבוּת לֵב 105
Generosity of spirit and giving way to others

26 עֲנָוָה—צְנִיעוּת וְהֶעְדֵּר יֵשׁוּת עַצְמִית 109
Humility and self-effacement

27 הַכָּרַת עַצְמוֹ 113
Recognizing one's own qualities

28 עֲשֵׂה לְךָ רַב—
הַצֹּרֶךְ בְּמוֹרֶה־דֶרֶךְ וּמַשְׁפִּיעַ בַּחַיִּים 116
The need in life for a guide and mentor

29 יֹקֶר הַזְּמַן 119
Appreciating the value of time

30 שְׁמִירָה מִפְּנֵי סַכָּנָה רוּחָנִית 123
Avoiding spiritual danger

31 שְׁמִירַת הַבְּרִיאוּת 127
Guarding one's health

PART THREE 133
Our Relationship with Others

32a אַהֲבַת יִשְׂרָאֵל 134
Love for a fellow Jew

32b הִמָּנְעוּת מִמְּרִיבוֹת—
לְעוֹלָם לֹא לָרִיב, בִּמְיֻחָד לֹא עַל מִצְווֹת 141
Never quarrel, especially over a *mitzvah*

33 צְדָקָה 143
Charity

34 הַכְנָסַת אוֹרְחִים 153
The *mitzvah* of hospitality

35a בִּקּוּר חוֹלִים 157
Visiting the sick

35b נִחוּם אֲבֵלִים 160
Comforting those in mourning

36 לֹא תַעֲמֹד עַל דַּם רֵעֶךָ—לֹא לַעֲמוֹד
בְּחֹסֶר מַעַשׂ כַּאֲשֶׁר דָּמוֹ שֶׁל מִישֶׁהוּ נִשְׁפָּךְ 163
Not standing idly by while the blood of one's fellow is being spilled

37 לָדוּן אֶת כָּל הָאָדָם לְכַף זְכוּת 165
Judging everyone favorably

38 אִסּוּר רְכִילוּת, לָשׁוֹן הָרָע, וּמוֹצִיא שֵׁם רָע 171
The prohibition against tale-bearing, gossip, and slander

39 עַיִן טוֹב—
שֶׁלֹּא לִרְאוֹת אֶת הָרַע וְהַשְּׁלִילִי בַּזּוּלַת 178
Not seeing the negative in another

40 "לֹא תִקֹּם" "לֹא תִטֹּר" 181
Not to take revenge. Not to hold a grudge

41 אִסּוּר הַלְבָּנַת פְּנֵי חֲבֵרוֹ—
לְהִמָּנַע מִלְּבַיֵּשׁ אֶת הַזּוּלָת 185
Not to embarrass another

42 מַרְאִית עַיִן—
שֶׁלֹּא לְהִתְנַהֵג בְּצוּרָה שֶׁנִּרְאֵית לֹא רְצוּיָה 189
Not to act in a way that appears sinful

43 אִסּוּר גְּנֵבָה וּגְזֵלָה 192
The prohibition against
theft and robbery

44 אִסּוּר גְּנֵבַת דַּעַת—שֶׁלֹּא לְהַטְעוֹת אוֹ לְרַמּוֹת 196
The prohibition against deception

45 "לֹא תַחְמֹד" וְ"לֹא תִתְאַוֶּה" 199
The prohibition against desiring
the possessions of another

46 אוֹנָאָה וְרַמָּאוּת 202
The prohibition against causing pain
to another by verbal deceit, hurting
another's feelings, or cheating

47 חֲנוּפָה 206
Flattery

48 הָאִסּוּר לְהַזִּיק אוֹ לִגְרוֹם
הֶזֵּק לְמָמוֹן שֶׁל חֲבֵרוֹ 210
The prohibition against damaging or
causing damage to another's property

49 הָאִסּוּר לְהַכּוֹת אֶת חֲבֵרוֹ 212
The prohibition against
striking one's fellow

50 "לִפְנֵי עִוֵּר לֹא תִתֵּן מִכְשֹׁל" 215
Not to place an obstacle before the blind

51 הֲשָׁבַת אֲבֵדָה 218
The requirement to return lost objects

PART FOUR 221

Our Relationship with the World

52 שְׁמִירָה מִפְּנֵי סַכָּנָה 222
Avoiding danger

53 בַּל תַּשְׁחִית—הָאִסּוּר לְאַבֵּד לָרִיק וּלְהַשְׁחִית 225
Not to be wasteful

54 הַצֹּרֶךְ לְהִתְחַבֵּר עִם אֲנָשִׁים טוֹבִים וּרְאוּיִים 228
The necessity to associate
with righteous people

55 שְׁמִירַת הָעֵינַיִם—
לְהִמָּנַע מִמַּרְאוֹת לֹא רְצוּיִים 232
Being careful what one looks at

56 שְׁתִיקָה—הִמָּנְעוּת מִדִּבּוּר מְיֻתָּר 235
Silence

57 טָהֳרַת הַדִּבּוּר 237
Purity of speech

58 שֵׁם שָׁמַיִם שָׁגוּר בְּפִיךָ—
לְהַזְכִּיר אֶת שֵׁם ה' תָּמִיד 241
To constantly mention the
Name of Heaven (G-d)

59 צַעַר בַּעֲלֵי חַיִּים"—
הָאִסּוּר לְצַעֵר בַּעֲלֵי חַיִּים וְלִפְגּוֹעַ בָּהֶם" 245
The prohibition against
causing harm to animals

60 צִפִּיָּה לִגְאֻלָּה 249
The imperative of awaiting the
coming of the Redemption and
the revelation of *Mashiach*

Index 255

Introduction

"לֹא נִתְּנָה הַתּוֹרָה אֶלָּא לְצָרֵף בָּהֶם אֶת הַבְּרִיּוֹת"—"The Torah was given in order to refine the person."[1]

Torah is the ultimate guide to life. It comprises not only the "written" and the "oral" law of *halachah*—G-d's instruction and guide how to live by keeping the *mitzvot*—but also instructs and guides a person how to live a life of **true values—the values that G-d Himself practices in His interactions with us.**

These are the less explicit but no less important Torah "laws" of personal refinement, proper character, and outlook—the true ideals to which each person should aspire.

Indeed, we are not only commanded to keep the *mitzvot*, but we are also commanded to "walk in the ways of Hashem"[2] (as is stated:[3] "And you shall walk in His ways").

Our Sages explained[4] this command to mean: "Just as He is called compassionate, so should you be compassionate and give freely," and so on.

In this way, the Torah is teaching us that the "ultimate" way to live, the ultimate "value" in life, is **a life of G-dly values**, to conduct ourselves as G-d conducts Himself.

---

1. *Tanchuma* on Leviticus 7:8. See *Likkutei Sichot*, vol. 25, p. 49; vol. 19, p. 182.

2. *Rambam, Sefer Hamitzvot, Mitzvat Asei*, where he lists the eighth mitzvah (*hamitzvah hasheminit*): "to walk in the ways of Hashem." See *Sefer Hachinuch, Mitzvah 611*. See *Shulchan Aruch Harav, Hilchot Masa Umatan* 156:3.

3. Deuteronomy 28:9.

4. *Shabbat* 133b (*Sotah* 14a).

Therefore, as part of the basic spiritual makeup of every Jew, belief in G-d requires us to acquire and develop "G-dly" values and character traits that exhibit goodness and upright behavior.[5]

Based on the way *Rambam* elucidates this *mitzvah*,[6] it is explained[7] that the goal is not so much the acquisition of these values and traits per se—although they are a good way to live and make sense—rather it is *to resemble Him.*

This means that our practice of mercy, compassion, and other similar traits follows not only the dictates of reason, which compel good and upright behavior, but rather because of our desire to emulate Hashem and *to resemble Him*—since these are **His** ways; knowing and believing in Hashem and His perfect nature inspires imitative action—conducting ourselves as G-d conducts Himself.

MUTUAL FAITH

A person should not think that this ideal of emulating Hashem is too high to achieve. If Hashem fashioned this principle of imitative behavior and emulation as a basis for our relationship with Him, this implies that He believes we can live up to it. So, as great as our faith in Him is [to the extent that we emulate Him], His faith in us is just as great, if not greater.

That is why we are instructed by the Torah to acquire those values and traits since in this way, we are indeed able to "imitate" our Creator and His Divine traits.

Furthermore, as servants of Hashem, who are constantly in His presence, standing before Hashem to serve Him[8] (as is stated:[9] "I place G-d in front of me, always"), we need to acquire the proper values of life, which include correct outlook,

5. In this way, one comes to know G-d in the truest sense.

6. Cited above, fn. 2.

7. *Likkutei Sichot*, vol. 34, pp. 156–158.

8. *Tanya*, ch. 41.

9. Psalms 16:8.

good character, and upright behavior as befitting a person chosen to attend and serve Hashem, the Creator and Director of the world.

All the more so does this apply to the Chasid—the servant of Hashem, whose entire outlook on life is directed by the drive to serve Hashem faithfully and with joy. It was R. Yosef Yitzchak Schneersohn, sixth Lubavitcher Rebbe, who, when defining what a Chasid is, said that along with other sterling traits and practices, a Chasid is a *middos tovos mentsch*—a person of good *middot*—good character traits and values.[10]

ABSOLUTE MORALS

The Torah does not command us to do something because it is moral. It is moral because the Torah commands it.

Over the generations, numerous books have been composed that explore and open up the world of Jewish values—good, truthful, and upright character traits, according to the Torah.

The novelty of this particular work, which is based in principle on *Rambam's Hilchot De'ot* (together with other sources), is to be found in its attempt to explore this world—but with an added dimension: how it is **illuminated by the inner light of Chasidic teachings**, many of which were quoted and expounded upon by the Lubavitcher Rebbe and are to be found in *Likkutei Sichot*.

Indeed, any characterization of this ideal would be incomplete without the insights of Chasidut.

Within this work, the reader will find not only *halachot* (laws) pertaining to behavior but will also find enumerated those desirable values—*middot* (character traits) and *de'ot* (mindset, attitudes) that are fitting for a Jew to acquire.

---

10. *Sefer Hasichot 5700*, p. 92.

These values fall into four categories, which mirror the four relationships we are all involved with on a daily basis—each one requiring the Torah's insight, instruction, and guidance—so that we may know how to live our lives truthfully, correctly, and successfully. Hence, the division of this work into four chapters:

1. ***Bein Adam l'Makom*—Our relationship with Hashem.**
2. ***Bein Adam l'Atzmo*—Our relationship with ourselves.**
3. ***Bein Adam l'Chavero*—Our relationship with others.**
4. ***Bein Adam l'Olam*—Our relationship with the world around us.**

Included within the text are numerous stories and examples of the conduct and customs of our great ancestors—those of Tanach, Talmudic Sages, righteous personalities, the early Chasidim, and "men of great deeds" down through the ages.

All were pedagogues of the highest caliber from whom there is much to learn, and even though we are not able to stand at their level and in their place, nevertheless, by keeping their example as our ideal and what to aim for in life, it will be possible for each of us to learn from their outlook and conduct many valuable life lessons for our own lives.

Their gift to us is the gift of their example—how one should think and behave.

In the spirit of the teaching of our Sages that **'Words written from the heart, enter the heart,'**[11] it is my prayerful wish that the material presented in this book will be of use to the many who seek to strengthen their connection to Hashem, and my heartfelt gratitude is offered to Hashem for granting me the

11. Based on Proverbs 27:19 (see *Metzudot David*), according to many opinions. See also *Berachot* 6b. Quoted in *Shirat Yisrael* by R. Moshe Ibn Ezra, p. 156.

opportunity to hopefully enrich the lives of others with the insights and teachings of the Torah on the topic of values—*de'ot* and *middot*—**Torah values for every person.**[12]

I wish to thank **Harav Yehuda Leib Schapiro**, *Rosh Yeshiva* of the *Yeshivah Gedolah of Greater Miami* and *Rav* of *Beis Haknesses Beis Menachem*, Miami Beach, Florida, for his moral support, encouragement, and help in the preparation of this book.

Also, my thanks to **Harav Levi Yitzchok Raskin**, Dayan and Rov of Kehillas Lubavitch, London, England, for checking the *halachah* in the original Hebrew text of the *Sefer Kitzur Halachot L'Avot Ubanim* from which this book is taken and for his many helpful suggestions.

Appreciation and thanks are due to the publishing team at Kehot Publication Society for their expertise and guidance in helping bring this project to fruition. Also, thanks to Moishe Muchnik, Zalman Friedman, Rachel Kaminetzky, and the Spotlight Team for their creative oversight, page styling, and cover design, and to Claudia Aumann for proofreading the text and for her helpful suggestions.

Although much effort has been expended to produce the best possible representation of the subject, should the reader have any comments, suggestions, or corrections, they would be welcomed by the author so that they may be incorporated into a subsequent edition.

Rabbi I. D. Silverman

---

12. This work is based on Rambam's *Hilchot De'ot*; *Kitzur Shulchan Aruch* §29-31; *Mishnah Avot*; *Tanya*, chs. 17, 18, and 41 and further sources in the *Tanya*; *Shulchan Aruch Harav* (*Hilchot Masa Umatan, Hilchot Nizkei Guf Venefesh, Hilchot Mechirah Umatanah* and more); *Likkutei Sichot*; and *Peleh Yoetz*. Also cited are numerous stories of *Tannaim* and *Amoraim* of the Talmud, plus stories of the Baal Shem Tov (as found in *Likkutei Sichot*) and early Chasidim from whom we can learn much about how a Jew should look at life and conduct himself.

PART ONE

Our Relationship with Hashem

1

אֱמוּנָה בַּה'

Belief in Hashem

The true reality of everything is G-dliness—Hashem's infinite and constant life-force that enlivens everything. The world is a façade—a mask that hides that truth. The key is to look beyond that which is superficial...to the G-dliness that pervades everything, to see that there is nothing but Hashem. This is the essence of the command *"I am the Lord your G-d..."*—the mitzvah of *emunah*—belief in Hashem, which is the first of the Ten Commandments and the ultimate expression of our connection to Hashem.

The essence of our faith and **the ultimate value** that lies at the very heart of Judaism is *emunat Hashem*—**belief in G-d**[1] (as commanded to us in the first of the Ten Commandments: "I am the Lord your G-d"—"***I***" indicating the existence of G-d).

Emunat Hashem **is the belief that it is He Who is the source of everything** (as stated in the verse:[2] "...for all is from You"), for **He created the world in six days and continues perpetually to create it from nothing at every instant**[3] (as stated in the verse:[4] "And You enliven all" and as we say every day in the blessings that precede the *Shema*: "...in His goodness He renews each day, continuously, the work of Creation").

Hashem's continuous re-creation of the world was a fundamental teaching of the Baal Shem Tov. Based on the verse[5] "Forever, G-d, Your word stands firm (and is enclothed) in Heaven," the Baal Shem Tov explained that **the original "saying" and "utterance" of G-d that created the vast Heavenly cosmos, continues to resound within it at every instant in order to enliven it from**

---

1. *Rambam, Sefer Hamitzvot*. Here, the term used by Rambam is to "**believe**" (*L'ha'amin*). In *Hilchot Yesodei Hatorah* 1:1, however, Rambam writes that the *mitzvah* is to "**know**" (*Leida*) that there is a *Matzui Rishon*—a Prime Cause to everything. Concerning this use of the two diverse terms, the Rebbe notes (see *Likkutei Sichot*, vol. 11, pp. 239 and 279, as well as numerous other references in *Likkutei Sichot*) that from the fact that ***Rambam*** uses both terms—"to believe" (in *Sefer Hamitzvot*) and "to know" (in *Hilchot Yesodei Hatorah*)—we can infer that that it is necessary to know of Hashem with the faculty of intellect (*biydiat hasechel*) as well as with *emunah*.

2. I Chronicles 29:14.

3. See *Shaar Hayichud VehaEmunah* ch. 2. See *Rambam* beginning *Hilchot Yesodei Hatorah*: "and He brings forth everything (i.e., creates everything *yesh mei'ayin*—from nothingness), and everything is from His true existence." See *Shaar Hayichud VehaEmunah* ch. 2, "...*Al tikra 'mechayeh' ela 'mehaveh'*"—"Do not read He 'gives life' rather He 'creates from nothing' (continuously)." See *Tanya*, Bi-Lingual edition, *Shaar Hayichud VehaEmunah* ibid., and the sources cited in the footnotes there. (Based on this teaching, that creation is a perpetual event, it could be said that the only reality is the moment of "now"—the current instant, which therefore should be used to accomplish something good and not wasted.)

4. Nehemiah 9:6.

5. Psalms 119:89.

nothingness, as the verse says:[6] "And the word of our Lord shall stand firm forever," and as we say every day in our prayers after the *Shema*: "...His words live and stand firm forever..." **So too, everything in creation exists only because of G-d's constant infusing life-force at every instant keeping it in existence.**

Thus, were Hashem to stop and disengage from the act of constant creation, even for an instant, Heaven forbid, everything would return to absolute nothingness since all of creation depends on G-d's constant investment within it in order to give it life and sustain it.

"EIYN OD MILVADO"—
THERE IS NOTHING
APART FROM HASHEM

R. Binyamin Kletzker was one of the great Chasidim of the Alter Rebbe and ran a large and successful timber enterprise. R. Binyamin was reviewing his profit and loss account, and when he came to the space provided for the *sach hakol*—the final and ultimate statement of his entire project—he entered the words *eiyn od milvado*—"There is nothing but Him."

It follows, then, that **the true reality of everything is Hashem's life-force**, and consequently, nothing truly exists apart from His life-force,[7] which is one with Him. This fundamental truth, which is at **the very heart of Judaism**, is expressed in the immortal words of Moshe to the Jewish people: Know this day...that *eiyn od*[8]—there is nothing aside from Hashem.

Due to its importance, *emunat Hashem*—belief in G-d—is the very **first** of the 613 commandments,[9] for through this faith, a person will come to fulfill all the 613 commandments.[10]

---

6. Isaiah 40:8.

7. Hashem's existence is totally independent. Creation's existence is therefore totally dependent. Thus, nothing exists in and of its own right. Therefore, Hashem's existence is the only totally true one. See *Likkutei Sichot*, vol. 34, p. 112, on this topic, where the Lubavitcher Rebbe relates the well-known story concerning R. Binyamin Kletzker.

8. Deuteronomy 4:35.

9. *Rambam, Sefer Hamitzvot, Mitzvat Asei: Hamitzvah Harishonah*—the "first *mitzvah*." See *Torat Menachem—Hitvaaduyot 5745*, vol. 3, p. 1766 ff.

10. See *Tanya*, ch. 33, explaining the saying of

It is the only *mitzvah* (together with the second of the Ten Commandments: "You shall have no gods beside Me"—both of which comprise the *mitzvah* of *emunah* in Hashem) **that we received directly from Hashem at Mount Sinai**, the remainder being transmitted via Moshe.[11]

It is for this reason perhaps that ***emunat Hashem,* above and beyond all other Jewish spiritual characteristics, is the one power we see most deeply rooted within every Jewish soul, being the ultimate expression of our connection to Hashem.**

EMUNAT HASHEM—THE DEEPEST POWER

The story told by the legendary Chasid and mentor R. Mendel Futerfas of his Yom Kippur experience in the Soviet gulag illustrates this point:

During the time R. Mendel was in a Soviet labor camp in Siberia, where he had been exiled for helping his coreligionists escape Soviet Russia in the dark days after World War II, he was taken away to the famous Spalerno prison-fortress in Leningrad, as it was known in those days, for questioning. This particular prison was the "model" prison in the Soviet system in that it allowed prisoners "exercise" time each day. They would walk around slowly in a big circle and were not allowed to stop or talk to each other.

One day, R. Mendel was walking in the exercise line, and it was Yom Kippur. (He knew this because he was always able to keep the calendar in his mind so that he should know when Shabbat, Rosh Chodesh, and Yom Tov would be.) As he walked along, he recited the prayers that he could remember from the Yom Kippur Machzor. Since much of the Yom Kippur prayers are said only once a year, it is hard to remember them, so he recited whatever he could remember, mostly the poems because they are easier to recall. As he began to say the prayer entitled "*V'chol Maaminim*" ("Everyone Believes"), there fell into his head a very strong question. How could it be that "everyone believes? It's patently untrue!" From the courtyard where he was walking, he looked up at all the cell windows of the prison.... "And here in this prison," he thought to himself, "who in those cells really believes? In the world, there are those who believe and those who don't. But to say that everyone believes...?"

However, he had learned early on in his *yeshivah* education a basic teaching of Chasidut: If a question

---

our Sages (*Makkot* 24a): "Six hundred and thirteen *mitzvot* were given to Israel; ...came Habakkuk and based them all on a single one—**faith**—as it is written (Habakkuk 2:4) "a *tzaddik* lives by his faith,' meaning that it is as if all the *mitzvot* consisted of this one *mitzvah* of faith alone, for **through faith alone, one will come to fulfill all the 613 *mitzvot*."**

11. *Makkot* 24a. See *Shaloh* beginning *parashat Yitro*. *Zohar* II, 276a. See *Tanya*, beginning ch. 20.

comes to you that troubles and interferes with your faith and you cannot find the answer to it at first, you should put it out of your mind, and in the merit of continuing on despite the question, Hashem will send the answer, somehow, and in His own time.

And so it was. A short time later, on Sukkot, he was in a big transit camp for prisoners on the way back to Siberia. As he was standing in the large barracks next to his bed praying, he sensed another prisoner at the end of the barracks looking at him very intensely. As R. Mendel finished his prayers, the other prisoner came toward him and introduced himself. As prisoners would do, they swapped their stories of how they ended up in prison. The other prisoner told R. Mendel that in one of Stalin's purges, the authorities had looked into his background, and it was found out that his grandfather had been a Chasid, a cardinal sin in those days, and he was sentenced to hard labor in Siberia.

He told R. Mendel: "Even though I am a communist and my father is a communist, I, nevertheless, kept this Yom Kippur." This puzzled R. Mendel because no one had a calendar in prison, so he asked him, "How did you know it was Yom Kippur?" The prisoner replied, "When I was in a cell in Spalerno, I heard a bang on the wall from the other side and someone called out in Yiddish from the next cell: '*Morgen iz Yom Kippur*—Tomorrow is Yom Kippur!' So I prayed all day!" This puzzled R. Mendel even more. "What did you pray?" he asked. The prisoner replied, "When I was very young, my grandfather would take me on his lap and teach me the *Modeh Ani* and the verse: *Torah tzivah lanu Moshe*...and that is what I said all day!"

From this, R. Mendel understood that the statement in the Machzor is indeed true—*V'chol Maamin-im*—every Jew believes! Even though it appears superficially that some may not believe, nevertheless, in essence, every Jew does indeed believe. This was the answer to his question.

The latent *emunat Hashem,* which is rooted within each Jewish soul going all the way back to the revelation at Mount Sinai, was brought to the surface through the seed of holiness and connection that was planted by the grandfather in his grandson, when he still a young child, staying with him for the rest of his life.

2

"שִׁוִּיתִי ה' לְנֶגְדִּי תָמִיד"

"I have placed Hashem before me constantly"—To live with the constant mindfulness of being in Hashem's presence at all times

---

The life G-d gives us is only truly lived if we are constantly mindful of Hashem's infinite Presence at all times.

Being that ***emunah* is our ultimate connection to Hashem, woven into the very fabric of our soul** (as explained above), it was therefore intended to be not just a "once-in-a-lifetime" or "occasionally used" attribute.

Not for this alone did Hashem Himself communicate the *mitzvah* of *emunat Hashem* to us directly at the giving of the Torah on Mount Sinai.

Hashem's intention was that it should be **lived every instant of life—we should live in a way that is a constant expression of this *emunah*.** Indeed, our soul longs to express this *emunah* constantly.

Therefore, the obligation of a Jew is to give it expression by fulfilling that which King David wrote in Psalms:[1] *Shiviti Hashem l'negdi tamid*—"I have placed Hashem before me *tamid*—constantly," by making Hashem's presence a living awareness—**living with the constant mindfulness that we are in Hashem's presence at all times.**[2]

It is for this reason that the *Shulchan Aruch*—the Code of Jewish Law—begins with this concept of *tamid*[3] by quoting right at its very beginning the above expression of King David: *Shiviti Hashem l'negdi tamid*, the need to

THE LESSON OF THE BA'AL SHEM TOV

The Ba'al Shem Tov revealed in King David's words: *Shiviti Hashem l'negdi tamid*—I have placed Hashem before me constantly—a technique how to bring oneself to live with this constant awareness of Hashem's presence. He taught that the term "***shiviti***" is the same terminology as "***hishtavut***," meaning **equal**. Everything can only be said to be equal when in comparison to Hashem, before Whom all is equally nothing. So with this mindset, that everything is really equal because it is in Hashem's Presence, a person comes to feel that he is in the presence of Hashem. **In this way, "*shiviti*" brings one to "*Hashem l'negdi tamid*."**

---

1. Psalms 16:8. See *Sanhedrin* 22a.

2. *Rama, Orach Chaim* 1:1. *Shulchan Aruch Harav* 1:5 (later edition) and 1:2 (earlier edition). *Tanya*, ch. 42.

3. See cources cited in the previous fn. See *Likkutei Sichot*, vol. 26, pp. 210-212.

be continuously focused and mindful that we are in Hashem's presence.[4]

In this way, we remember our unique calling in life as Hashem's servants, charged with creating a dwelling place for His presence in this world through Torah and *mitzvot*, as set out in the *Shulchan Aruch*.

With this mindfulness of Hashem's presence, therefore, a person is able to live life connected to Hashem. In practice, the way to achieve this is to stay focused and not let secondary "attractions" divert us from this mindfulness.[5]

LIVING WITH THE CONSTANT MINDFULNESS OF HASHEM'S PRESENCE TAKES FOCUS

The importance of focus in attaining the spiritual goals of life and the dangers inherent in losing that focus are illustrated in the well-known story told by R. Mendel Futerfas that describes another of his experiences in a Russian forced-labor camp.

The story occurred in 1953, a short time after the death of Stalin, the Russian leader. Having been a tyrant, great relief was felt on his demise, not only among the prisoners but also among the camp administration, so a "holiday" was declared in the camp—one day on which no one would have to work. Instead, a "show" was arranged. Each prisoner would exhibit some particular talent that he possessed and share it with the other prisoners. A singer would sing. An artist would draw. A joker would tell jokes. And so on.

One such prisoner had worked previously in a circus and was a tightrope walker. He strung up a wire between two buildings and walked across. This fascinated R. Mendel, and he asked the performer how he did it. The tightrope walker replied that it was not as hard as it looked. The key was to stay focused on the goal you are aiming at with 100% of your being and then you will not fall down. If you look down to this side or the other, you are finished, and you are going to fall off the rope. The only

4. There is a second *tamid* in Jewish life (hinted to in the command of G-d to offer two *temidim*—two continuous offerings each day (Exodus 29:38))—and that is one with which the *Shulchan Aruch, Orach Chaim*, concludes (§597) and that is the *tamid* of King Solomon, who said (Proverbs 15:15): *Tov leiv mishteh tamid*—a happy heart is a constant feast. Keeping the *mitzvot* as set out in the *Shulchan Aruch* imbues everything we do with G-dly significance and meaning, thus bringing the joy of meaning and purpose into life. (See *Rambam, Hilchot Lulav* 8:15. See *Tanya* ch. 33. See *Likkutei Sichot* ibid., p. 211, fn. 18. See *Torat Menachem—Hitvaaduyot*, vol. 54, p. 213.)

5. Anything that takes a person away from the awareness of Hashem's presence is a distraction and ultimately a denial of our purpose in life.

hard bit is the turn at the end to walk back because your focus is taken off the goal for an instant and switched around.

When he heard this, R. Mendel recalled the teaching of the Ba'al Shem Tov, who said that everything that one hears or sees in life is by Divine providence and contains some life lesson in *avodat Hashem*—how to better connect to Hashem and serve Him.

So it is in life, said R. Mendel. Life is like walking along a tightrope. As long as you keep 100% focused on your goal, then you will not fall. As soon as you become distracted, you can fall.

3

הַשְׁגָּחָה פְּרָטִית—הָאֱמוּנָה בְּהַשְׁגָּחָה אֱלוֹקִית עַל הַכֹּל

Belief in Divine Providence

Hashem, the Creator of all things, is aware of and actively supervises every detail of His creation from its greatest and most magnificent aspects down to the minutest details. He sees the "big" picture as well as the "small" picture at the same time. He runs the entire world and at the same time concentrates on the needs of each individual, orchestrating every detail to ensure that everything He has created plays an irreplaceable part in His overall plan and purpose for the entire creation.

Belief in Hashem as the Creator of all things includes, by implication, belief in His individual providence over every aspect of creation, referred to as *hashgachah pratit*.

This is the belief that Hashem, Who perpetually creates the world from nothingness at every moment, is aware of and actively supervises every detail of the creation, from its greatest and most magnificent aspects down to the individual motions of each created being.

In this vein, the Baal Shem Tov taught that even a blade of grass, as it turns and sways in the wind, is doing so because of *hashgachah pratit*—having been so decreed in Heaven.[1]

It is explained[2] that if this is so with a "lowly" blade of grass, then certainly this applies to the "grander" affairs of man, whose every issue and every need is governed by divine providence.[3]

(We affirm this each morning in our prayers when we say the paragraph commencing *ezrat avoteinu*: "In the heights of the universe is Your dwelling place, and Your judgment and righteousness extend to the ends of the earth.")

Our calling in life is to sensitize our

TO KNOW AND TO SEE

A Chasidic saying that encapsulates this concept says: "A *yoshev ohel*—one who inhabits the world of Torah learning—**knows** that G-d runs the world. A *ba'al eisek*—one who inhabits the world of business—**sees** that G-d runs the world."

1. *Keter Shem Tov (Hosafot)* §125. See *Radak* on the verse in Psalms (148:8): *Ruach sa'arah oseh devaro*—"the stormy wind fulfills His word" explaining that every move of the wind is a fulfillment of G-d's word and command.

2. *Sefer Hamaamarim Kuntresim*, vol. 2, p. 740.

3. See *Igrot Kodesh by R. Yosef Yitzchak*, vol 3, p. 112, where this is explained based on the verse in Psalms (37:23): *MeiHashem mitzadei gever konanu*—"The steps of man are set by G-d." In a similar vein, R. Shmuel, fourth Lubavitcher Rebbe, said that the phrase "If I would have..." is actually heresy and a denial of the entire concept of *hashgachah pratit*.

minds and hearts so that we are able, as a matter of habit, to see Hashem's involvement in all things and all occurrences.[4] **This brings us to realize that, while He renews the entire world at every moment, "hand in hand" with this, in His kindness, He is concerned with the affairs of each individual being.**

So, while a mortal king cannot look at the "**big** picture" (the general or global picture) and the "**small** picture" (the individual details) at the same time,[5] G-d, however, is able to, and indeed, does both at the same time: **He runs the world and at the same time concentrates on the needs of each individual.**[6]

Furthermore, it is explained[7] that in addition to G-d's awareness and supervision over every aspect of the creation, belief in divine providence encompasses the belief that **each individual and each part of the creation plays an irreplaceable role in, and contributes to, G-d's overall plan and purpose for creation as a whole**—this is especially so with the Jewish people whose service of Hashem is the ultimate purpose of creation.

In other words, not only does Hashem

ADON OLAM

The prayer *Adon Olam* that we say each day expresses one of our core beliefs. In it, we commence by praising Hashem as *Adon Olam*—the Master of the Universe—and end by saying *vehu Keili v'chai goali*—"He is **my** G-d and **my** living Redeemer"—**universal** yet **personal, infinite yet intimate**. This foundation of Jewish monotheism is the source from which we derive our belief in the power and efficacy of prayer.

BIRTHDAY

An insight of the Rebbe on the topic of birthdays relates to this concept: "A person's birthday is the anniversary of the day on which G-d decided that the world could no longer exist without them."

4. *Igrot Kodesh by R. Yosef Yitzchak*, vol. 4, p. 548. *Hayom Yom*, 29 *Sivan*.

5. *Bereishit Rabbah* 9:3.

6. This belief that G-d is universal yet personal stands at the center of Jewish monotheism.

7. *Likkutei Sichot*, vol. 30, p. 149. See there, p. 150, where the explanation of the concept of *hashgacha pratit* according to the Baal Shem Tov is elucidated. See *Shaar Hayichud VehaEemunah* ch. 2. *Likkutei Sichot*, vol. 8, p. 277, "*Reshimat Hashgacha Pratit.*"

supervise each and every individual creation in particular, He also relates to every individual as an integral part of the entire scheme of creation.

4

לְמּוֹד הוֹרָאָה מִכָּל דָּבָר
שֶׁרוֹאִים אוֹ שׁוֹמְעִים

To learn a life lesson from everything one sees or hears

The Baal Shem Tov taught that Hashem does not just bring us into life and then leave us. He remains with us as life's Great Guide and Teacher, and His lessons guide us through life constantly. Therefore, since every life experience comes from Hashem, each one comes with a precious gift—an inbuilt, tailor-made, and thoughtfully designed life-lesson how best to fulfill our purpose in life. Every experience therefore has within it the potential to lift us higher and bring us nearer to Hashem.

The Baal Shem Tov taught[1] that an integral part of belief in Hashem and His providence is the belief that **every event** we encounter in life, whatever we see or hear, is also a part of the divine plan for the universe and therefore must contain a **life lesson** for us in our life mission, which is *avodat Hashem*—the service of G-d.

Our task is to look upon these events as **teaching experiences** from which we should draw insight and instruction how best to serve Hashem. The Sages said:[2] "G-d created nothing in His world in vain," rather, "everything is for His glory,"[3] and therefore, if the Holy One, blessed is He, caused a person to see some occurrence or hear of some matter, then that is not for naught but for a distinct purpose, namely, the purpose of man's creation: *avodat Hashem*, as the Sages said, "I was created to serve my Creator."[4]

Therefore, **every experience has within it the potential to lift us higher and bring us nearer to Hashem** through the life lesson it can teach us.

We find an example of this from a well-known story[5] that teachers have traditionally related to their young students involving the famous medieval commentator on the Torah—Rashi.

On the Torah portion of *Tetzaveh*, Rashi writes that the *ephod* worn by the high priest is "like the apron worn

---

1. See *Keter Shem Tov* §127-129 (§126) and the footnotes there. See *Hayom Yom*, 9 *Iyar*. See *Igrot Kodesh by R. Yosef Yitzchak*, vol. 2, p. 538, where the story is told of a dream in which his father, the Rebbe Rashab, reminds him of the teaching of the Baal Shem Tov that "**every word a Jew hears is in truth the word of G-d, and** contains a lesson in *avodat Hashem*...."

2. *Shabbat* 77a.

3. *Avot* 6:11.

4. *Kiddushin* 4:14.

5. Quoted in *Likkutei Sichot*, vol. 26, p. 198.

by noblewomen when they ride horses," which is an example not necessarily known to the average reader (and certainly not to the "five-year-old student being introduced to the written text,"[6] which is the mind-set of innocence, clarity, pure logic, and freshness of thought that Rashi used as his measure to meet when formulating his commentary). Such students would have no knowledge of this type of apron worn by noblewomen, especially as it is not explained elsewhere. Why, then, would Rashi use such an obscure illustration, and what is Rashi's source?

To clarify this enigma, teachers in times gone by would relate the following story:

Rashi was always meticulous in guarding his eyesight from seeing things that could lessen his spiritual clarity. Once, he was out walking and saw a noblewoman riding a horse dressed in an apron. He was troubled why this had happened to him and questioned why Hashem would want him to see it.

Some time later, when he wrote his commentary on the Torah regarding the *ephod*, he was comforted. Rashi realized that he had been shown the noblewoman riding the horse in order to better understand the *ephod* so that he could clarify it in his commentary (even to a "five-year-old being introduced to the written text").

This story concerning Rashi illustrates the Baal Shem Tov's teaching that everything a Jew sees or hears is planned and purposeful in order to help us serve Hashem, whether it be through study of Torah, the performance of *mitzvot*, or using the mundane daily

6. See *Klolei Rashi* (R. Tuvya Blau) p. 81 and the sources cited there. (See *Avot* 5:22.)

material things of life we come into contact with for the sake of Heaven, i.e., to fulfill Hashem's will.

Another example of the Baal Shem Tov's teaching on the lessons of divine providence involved the Baal Shem Tov himself.[7]

Once, while he was studying with his disciples, a non-Jew passed by and requested their help. The disciples replied that they were unable to help. To this, the non-Jew responded "You are able, but you don't want to" and went away.

Witnessing this, the Baal Shem Tov said to the students that words of the passerby contain a great lesson in the service of Hashem: "If one doesn't **want to**, then it appears as if one is **unable to**. Really, every Jew is truly able to serve G-d...if only one wants to—it's up to us...." From this story, too, we see that everything a Jew hears, even from a non-Jew, can teach us a lesson in the service of G-d.

Accordingly, a person is obligated to learn a lesson from everything and to know that everything one sees or hears is sent from Above and for good reason. This is a cornerstone of our belief. Hashem does not just bring us into life and then leave us. He remains with us as life's Great Teacher, and His lessons guide us through life.

7. See *Igrot Kodesh by R. Yosef Yitzchak*, vol. 9, p. 98. See *Torat Menachem—Hitvaaduyot*, vol. 21, p. 134; vol. 28, p. 239.

5

"אֵין רָע יוֹרֵד מִלְמַעְלָה"
– שׁוּם דָּבָר שְׁלִילִי לֹא בָּא מֵאֵת ה׳
No negativity descends from Heaven

Seeing good as the inner essence of every situation reveals the latent good that Hashem has placed within all life experiences.

All of man's experiences come from G-d by divine providence, as explained above. **Since G-d is the epitome of goodness, it is therefore impossible that those experiences should be "bad,"**[1] as the Sages say:[2] "All that the Merciful One does, He does for the good."

For this reason, even when a person's situation seems the opposite of good (G-d forbid), in truth, the apparent negativity is just in the "wrapping." Inwardly, however, and in essence, the situation is good,[3] **and with the right perspective, one can discern how what we perceive as "negative" works out in the end positively.**

A story concerning R. Akiva, as told in the Talmud,[4] exemplifies this teaching: R. Akiva was once traveling and reached a city as nightfall was approaching. He requested lodgings but was denied by the people of the city. So he told himself, "All that the Merciful One does, He does for the good," and he went to sleep in a field.

He had with him a rooster to wake him, a donkey, and a candle. A wind came and blew out the candle, a cat came and ate the rooster, and a lion came and devoured the donkey. At each occurrence, R. Akiva repeated, "All that the Merciful One does, He does for the good."

That very night, bandits came, attacked the city, and ransacked it. R. Akiva realized that having been refused hospitality in the city and ending up out in the field was in fact a kindness. Similarly, losing his light so that he was not visible to the bandits and losing his

---

1. *Iggeret Hakodesh*, 11.
2. *Berachot* 60b (see *Taanit* 21a).
3. See *Likkutei Sichot*, vol. 1, p. 284.
4. See *Likkutei Sichot* there, fn. 2.

animals that could make noise and attract attention—all this was in the end for the good. R. Akiva then repeated, "Did I not say, all that the Merciful one does, He does for the good?"

There is a second story in the Talmud[5] on this topic, one that demonstrates an even higher level of faith:

Nachum Ish Gamzu was sent on behalf of the Jewish people to bring a chest of diamonds as a gift to the king of Rome. At an inn on the way, thieves stole the fine gems and replaced them with earth. When Nachum Ish Gamzu realized what had happened, he was not crestfallen but, on the contrary, said, "*Gam zu letovah*—This, too, is for the good."

When Nachum Ish Gamzu came before the king and the chest was opened revealing the earth, the king thought he was being insulted by the Jews and flew into a rage, wishing to kill Nachum Ish Gamzu and all the Jews. Yet again, Nachum Ish Gamzu said, "*Gam zu letovah*—This, too, is for the good."

As a reward for this refined level of trust, G-d then sent Elijah the Prophet, who appeared as one of the ministers attending the Roman king, and said, "Surely this must be special earth, perhaps that of Abraham, who would throw earth at his enemies, which would then rain down on them as spears and arrows."

The Romans decided to test Nachum's earth on a city that they were eager to conquer, and they found that it was indeed miraculous. In this merit, the king became

---

5. *Taanit* 21a. *Sanhedrin* 108b.

favorably disposed to the Jews and sent them in return a chest full of precious stones.

It is explained[6] that there is a subtle, yet deep, difference between the stories of R. Akiva and Nachum Ish Gamzu:

What happened to R. Akiva was ostensibly negative and painful, but through this suffering, he was preserved from what would have been worse, and thus, Hashem did "for the good"—G-d's seemingly negative acts were for good ends.

Nachum Ish Gamzu, however, saw that what initially seemed negative was itself good since the miraculous earth certainly pleased the king, while the diamonds may not have. This is why Nachum said, "This, too, is for the good," for he understood that the good was simply hidden.

Thus, seeing good as the inner essence of every situation reveals the latent good that G-d has planted in all life experiences.

6. *Likkutei Sichot*, vol. 2, p. 395.

6

לְבָרֵךְ עַל הָרָע כְּשֵׁם שֶׁמְּבָרְכִים עַל הַטּוֹב

The obligation to bless G-d for the "negative" as well as for the "positive"

Hashem is the source of all events. Whether it be "trial" or "triumph," it's all from Him, and both come with blessing, so even the tribulations of life can serve to connect us to Hashem rather than distance us from Him.

Our Sages state[1]: **Just as one is obligated to bless G-d for the "good," so too should one bless G-d for the "bad."**

We might wonder **how it is possible to thank G-d for the "trials" of life with the same joy as for the "triumphs" of life?**

It is explained[2] that since all events come from Hashem, Who is the epitome of goodness (as explained above), **it is impossible for them to be anything but good, which is line with the saying of our Sages[3] that "no negativity descends from Heaven."**

For this reason, it is understood that even in a situation that seems bad, it is inappropriate to complain; in the words of R. Akiva: "All that the Merciful One does, He does for the good."[4] Therefore, even when Hashem's treatment of man appears to be the opposite of good (Heaven forbid), it is perforce positive (as in the stories quoted above), and one should therefore bless Hashem equally for the "negative," just as one blesses Him for the "positive."

FOR THE "GOOD" AND FOR THE APPARENTLY "NOT SO GOOD"—THANK YOU

Just as a person says *Hodu l'Hashem ki tov ki l'olam chasdoh*—"Give thanks to Hashem for He is kind, His kindness is forever" when something that is positive ("revealed" good) happens, so too when something supposedly negative ("hidden good") happens, a person should say to himself, "I believe that this is for my good," for it is in order to bring me nearer to Hashem through my understanding that this is coming from Him (for there is only one G-d, from Whom everything comes). In this way, a person rises above the test and connects to Hashem at an even higher level than prior to the test. Furthermore, if there is pain or suffering involved (G-d forbid), then this can eradicate previous sins, and thereby also a person comes nearer to Hashem, for those sins no longer separate between him and Hashem.

A Chasidic story concerning R. Zusha of Hanipol[5] expresses this principle. The Maggid of Mezritch once sent a student to the destitute and suffering R. Zusha to learn how to accept

1. *Berachot* 9:5.
2. *Igeret Hakodesh*, 11.
3. *Bereishit Rabbah* 15:3.
4. See above, page 30.
5. Quoted in *Likkutei Sichot*, vol. 4, p. 1081.

suffering with joy. When the student arrived to R. Zusha and conveyed the purpose of his visit, R. Zusha replied that he didn't understand how he could teach the student to accept suffering with joy since he personally suffered no troubles and lacked nothing!

With this outlook in mind, a person is able to bless and thank Hashem for the "negative" as well as for the "positive."

This is in line with the teaching of the Baal Shem Tov on the verse in Psalms,[6] *Shiviti Hashem l'negdi tamid* (literally: I have placed Hashem before me constantly): The word *shiviti,* he pointed out, is the same terminology as the word *shavah*—equal—whether it's good (i.e., revealed good) or what appears to be the opposite of good (i.e., hidden good), it's all equal because it all comes from Hashem.[7]

This awareness, that everything comes from Hashem, creates the mindset called *hishtavut* (from the word *shavah*) meaning equanimity—mental calmness and composure in all situations, which is only possible when one knows that everything comes from Hashem.

Furthermore, with this belief, a person is able to "accept tribulations with love." If, instead of complaining and succumbing to anger or to sadness as a result of one's apparently "bad lot" in life, a person believes that the difficulty he is going through is planned with great exactitude and kindness by Hashem (since this

---

6. Psalms 16:8. See *Tzavaat Harivash* §2 for elucidation of the the Baal Shem Tov's teaching concerning *hishtavut,* based on this verse. See *Vayikra Rabbah* 25:2 on King David's words (Psalms 56:11): *BeElokim ahallel daver, baHashem ahallel davar*—Whether its *chesed* or what appears to be the opposite—"either way, I will praise His word."

7. *Igrot Kodesh by the Lubavitcher Rebbe,* vol. 19, p. 257. Therefore, a good guiding principle in life before rushing to judge any situation would be: "Wait and see...."

is a manifestation of Hashem's just and faithful providence and must therefore be kindness), then a person will be able to accept these trials and tribulations with "love" (or at the very least with equanimity).

In this way, the "tribulations" of life can serve to connect us to Hashem rather than distance us from Him.

7

בִּטָּחוֹן בַּה'

Trust in Hashem

Emunah is that Hashem **can** provide for, help, and rescue us. *Bitachon* is that Hashem **will** do so. *Bitachon* itself elicits Hashem's salvation measure for measure as a reward for placing, without worry, our complete trust in Hashem. Hence, the advice, *Tracht gut, vet zein gut*—"Think good, and it will be good."

Faith (*emunah*) in G-d's individual providence (as explained above) brings a person to "trust" (*bitachon*).

***Emunah* is that Hashem "can," while *bitachon* is that Hashem "will."**

We are commanded[1] not only to have faith in Hashem—in His **ability** to watch over, provide for, and rescue from harm every individual—but also to trust in Him that **He will, in fact, do so.**

How does *emunah* bring one to *bitachon*?

It is explained[2] that there is an additional element to our *emunah*:

Every Jew has, in addition to Hashem's individual providence over **all** of creation, a **personal** connection with the Holy One, blessed is He, that transcends nature. This relationship is analogous to the bond between a son with his father, as the verse says:[3] "You are sons to Hashem, your G-d." As a result of His choice of the Jewish people as His people, G-d watches over and relates to every Jew as a father who loves his children, and this bond transcends all limitation.

Although a father and son do have a superficial and "measured" relationship, wherein the father desires to educate and raise his son correctly and therefore rewards and punishes the son according to the son's actions, this is, however, only their **"external"** relationship.

---

1. See the sources cited in *Likkutei Sichot*, vol. 36, p. 3, fn. 27 and p. 5, fn. 41.

2. See *Torat Menachem—Sefer Hamaamarim 5712*, p. 321 ff.

3. Deuteronomy 14:1.

There is also a profound **"internal"** relationship between them, which surpasses any reasoning or logic and is not dependent upon the son's actions. When this deep connection is awakened, such as during a time of unusual joy or, G-d forbid, sorrow, the father treats his son with great kindness, beyond the measure of any justification.

So, too, in our relationship with Hashem: Our faith in Him as our Master, and specifically as our Father, assures us that He **will** treat us with a transcendental kindness due to our deep bond with Him.

However, as in the analogy, this internal bond must be awakened when we, the Jewish people, reveal our profound connection to G-d through our *bitachon*, being sure that because of this deep "father-son" relationship, His kindness toward us will far transcend any measure of what we may deserve, then this *bitachon* itself awakens G-d's fatherly compassion and generates the salvation that we seek.

So, *bitachon* itself elicits G-d's open kindness, which transcends reason, based on the principle of "measure for measure."[4] When a Jew has complete trust in G-d, that is, a Jew relies upon G-d alone, this itself elicits from Heaven G-d's infinite kindness[5] (even if in the ledger of good and bad deeds, he may be undeserving[5]) **to the extent that a person can, through trust, transform even "bad" decrees into open and revealed good.[6]**

This was the advice of R. Menachem Mendel, third Lubavitcher Rebbe and author of *Tzemach Tzedek*, to a

---

4. *Sotah* 8b.

5. *Likkutei Sichot* ibid., fn. 40.

6. *Likkutei Sichot* ibid., fn. 43.

certain distressed Jew: *Tracht gut, vet zein gut*—"Think good, and it will be good."[7] This phrase implies that the good thought itself (the *bitachon* itself) brings about good results. In other words, Hashem's kindness is a consequence of, and a reward for, man's efforts to rely on and trust in G-d (even in situations that demand supernatural salvation).[8]

When in the depths of our souls we truly trust and rely on G-d, to the extent that we are not even worried, then this elicits from G-d the salvation we seek, as explained above (and with this in mind, a wise man once counseled: **"Don't be a worrier...be a warrior!"**).

In this vein, King David said in Psalms,[9] "He who trusts in Hashem will be encircled with kindness," teaching us that he who trusts in Hashem will see the kindness and salvation that comes as a result.[10]

The greater the trust, therefore, the more a person sees the *hashgachah*—the active help and intervention of Hashem. Conversely, the weaker the trust and the more

7. *Likutei Dibburim* 1, p. 159. *Igrot Kodesh by R. Yosef Yitzchak*, vol. 2, p. 537; vol. 7, p. 197. See *Igrot Kodesh by the Lubavitcher Rebbe*, vol. 3, p. 364, where proof is suggested from the Talmud to this concept of "Think good and it will be good."

8. See *Likkutei Sichot*, vol. 36, p. 3, fn. 31. In our daily prayers (*Uvah l'Tzion*) we mention the verse from Jeremiah (17:7): *Baruch hagever asher yivtach baShem vehayah Hashem mivtacho*—"Blessed is the man who trusts in Hashem, and Hashem is his trust." The Baal Shem Tov taught that the first part, "Blessed is the man who trusts in Hashem," refers to one who needs Hashem's salvation but appears to have a "backup" solution. The second part, "and Hashem is his trust," is not a repetition of the first stanza. Rather, it refers to one who does not have, or does not create, a "backup" solution, for he trusts implicitly in Hashem. This elicits the salvation he seeks from Heaven (the *Tzemach Tzedek*, in *Pelach Harimon* 62c). And this is what King David was alluding to when he asked (Psalms 121:1): *...**me'ayin** yavo ezri?*, literally, "**from where** will my help come?", which can also be read as "***me'ayin***," meaning "**from nothing**"—"**from the unseen and hidden** (i.e., Hashem) will come my help," as the verse continues: *ezri me'im Hashem*—"my help is from Hashem."

9. Psalms 32:10.

10. See *Peleh Yoetz, Havtachah*. (How we approach each day is up to us: we can allow anxiety to color our perception of what is ahead, or we can go to the day with trust in Hashem.)

that a person relies on nature, the less that person sees Hashem's open *hashgachah,* which is consequently withdrawn, leaving him vulnerable to the laws of nature.

THE POWER OF BITACHON

In biblical times, those who were fearful of battle were instructed to leave the army before the fighting commenced because the entire success of the Jewish army was predicated upon the degree of trust that the soldiers had in Hashem, not upon their military power. On the contrary, their *bitachon* **was** their power. A soldier lacking *bitachon* and therefore was fearful was thus open to capture or worse. This is what Isaiah the prophet referred to when he wrote (Isaiah 30:15): "In quiet trust will be your power." Similarly, King David wrote (Psalms 118:6): "Hashem is with me, I have no fear, what can a man do to me?"

8

אַל יִאוּשׁ—לְעוֹלָם לֹא לְאַבֵּד אֶת הַתִּקְוָה

Never lose hope

Never lose hope. There is no place for despair in Jewish life. A person always has prayer. The power of heartfelt prayer is infinite and breaks through all barriers.

Based on the power of *bitachon* (as explained above), **it can be understood that there is no room for a Jew to ever lose the hope and trust that salvation can come.**

Our Sages tell us[1] that one of the first questions that we will be asked when we come before the Heavenly Tribunal after our life in this world will be *Tzipita liyeshuah*?—literally, "Did you yearn for the redemption?"

However, this can also be interpreted to express the idea of expecting salvation in a more personal way: Did you, when faced with the difficulties that you went through during the course of your lifetime, expectantly and optimistically await salvation?

Our Sages say,[2] "Even if a sharp sword is at a man's neck, he must not despair of Hashem's mercy."

We learn this from a story in the Talmud[3] concerning King Hezekiah, upon whom Hashem brought sickness due to his decision not to marry and have children. The king foresaw that if he had children, they would turn out to be wicked and would lead the people away from G-d, bringing destruction upon the nation as a result.

G-d sent the prophet Isaiah to tell the king that he would die. When asked why, the prophet answered that it was because of his decision to refrain from having children. When Hezekiah told him that the reason was because of what he foresaw, the prophet scolded him, telling him that he had no business meddling in G-d's hidden affairs. He, Hezekiah, was commanded to have children; let G-d do what He thinks fit to do.

---

1. *Shabbat* 31a.
2. *Berachot* 10a.
3. Ibid.

Hezekiah proposed that Isaiah give him his daughter to marry in the hope that the merit of both of them, Isaiah and Hezekiah, would bring good merit to their offspring. Isaiah, however, replied: "It has already been decreed that you will die."

Hezekiah retorted: "Son of Amotz, end your prophecy and leave! I have received a tradition from the house of my father's father (from King David) that 'even if a sharp sword is on a man's neck, he should not despair of Hashem's mercy.'"

Hezekiah then turned to face the wall and prayed. When G-d heard his supplications, he sent Isaiah back to the king to tell him that G-d would add fifteen years to his life.

From this story, we learn that there is no room for despair in the life of a Jew, and we must never lose hope (it is said that the worst impediment in life is despair and loss of hope[4])—the power of heartfelt prayer is infinite and breaks through all barriers, eliciting salvation from Heaven even when all hope seems lost.[5]

---

4. There is a well-known dictum called *yiush shelo midaat*. This is a halachic term referring to the dissociation between a lost object and its owner when the owner is unaware of his loss. However, the Hebrew term literally reads as "giving up hope unawares." This is explained to imply that all "*yiush*"—all despair—results from "*shelo midaat*"—lack of knowledge—i.e., when one forgets that everything is from Heaven and is therefore for the good. If that awareness is gone or forgotten, a person despairs (*Torat Menachem—Hitvaaduyot 5743*, vol. 4, p. 261). See also *Igrot Kodesh by the Lubavitcher Rebbe* as listed in its subject index. (See also the Chasidic saying quoted by R. Mendel Futerfas, mentioned below, end of section 16.)

5. The power of prayer to reach so far is compared to an arrow. Whereas Torah is compared to a sword (see *Rashi* on Genesis 48:22) that is effective at close range (but the weapon remains with the person in his hand for future use), prayer, on the other, hand is compared to a bow that shoots an arrow that can reach very far, much farther than a sword, although once expended for one target, a new "arrow" is needed for the next target (*Maskil LeDavid* based on *Sotah* 21a and *Berachot* 32b).

9

מִדָּה כְּנֶגֶד מִדָּה
—כָּךְ הִיא הַנְהָגַת הַקָּדוֹשׁ
בָּרוּךְ הוּא עִם הָאָדָם

Measure for measure

The "upper" and the "lower" worlds work in tandem. Every action of ours in this world, whether positive or negative, has far-reaching effects and brings about, "measure for measure," a similar reaction from "Above."

Faith in Hashem and His ways includes the faith that G-d's justice and faithfulness are perfect[1]—each "cause" producing G-d's measured "effect," for Hashem interacts with man in a manner of measure for measure.[2] That is, just as man behaves below, so does G-d treat him from Above. The two worlds—the upper and the lower—work in tandem.

This is the explanation of what King David said in Psalms,[3] "Hashem is your shadow"—Just as a person's shadow follows his motions, so does the Holy One, blessed is He, deal with a person according to his actions. Consequently, a person should be aware that **every action, whether positive or negative, brings about a similar reaction from "Above."[4]**

(In truth, there is great kindness in this system of measure for measure: Since nothing is random and every "effect" can be traced back to a "cause," it enables a person (a) to do *teshuvah* and repair some past deed needing repair and do so right at its source and (b) it spurs a person on to greater good when the positive results of previous good actions become apparent.)

1. Psalms 18:31.

2. *Sotah* 1:7. See *Sotah* 8b and 11a. See *Rashi* on Exodus 18:11—we see that this system of "measure for measure" works not only on a personal level but also on a national level, especially for those nations that interact with the Jewish people.

3. Psalms 121:5.

4. See *Likkutei Sichot*, vol. 16, p. 201, fn. 73: *Yitro's* whole belief in Hashem came about precisely because of this principle of measure for measure. If G-d would have destroyed the Egyptians at the splitting of the sea in any other way (not through water, which was the weapon they themselves had used against the Jews), then that would have indeed ascribed power to G-d as being a G-d stronger than nature. In other words, nature has its own power, but G-d is more powerful. To have destroyed the Egyptians with the one thing that they attempted to destroy the Jews with—"measure for measure"—showed that everything, including nature, is just a tool in Hashem's hand. Nature has no intrinsic power of its own. It is, like everything in creation, a tool in Hashem's hand—the glove within which is the hand of Hashem.

10

אֵין הַקָּבָּ"ה מְבַקֵּשׁ אֶלָּא לְפִי כֹּחַ שֶׁל כָּל אֶחָד וְאֶחָד

G-d requests from each one only according to his ability

If Hashem has requested some act from us, or some good deed comes our way, this itself is proof that we have the potential and the ability to perform it. With this insight, we can rise to every challenge.

Underlying each person's service of Hashem through the performance of the *mitzvot* is the belief that since the *mitzvot* are Hashem's commandments and directives to each and every person, it is undoubtedly possible to fulfill them. **If Hashem requested some act from us or some good deed comes our way, this itself is proof that we have the potential and the ability to rise to the challenge and do it.**

In matters of serving Hashem, it can be tempting to say that we do not have the ability to perform this or that *mitzvah*, this or that good deed, or undertake a new and significant project. However, this is a misguided approach that leads to inertia and is simply not true.[1]

The truth is, and this is a great and abiding principle in life, that someone who desires to do good not only has the ability to do good (as is said concerning spiritual matters, that "Nothing stands in the way of a strong will"[2]) but will be actually helped by Hashem to accomplish that good intention.

When we begin to fulfill a *mitzvah*, we draw down upon ourselves Heavenly assistance, as is written in the Talmud,[3] "One who desires to become impure (that is, to sin, G-d forbid), the way is open for him," that is, it is only "open"; man is neither helped nor prevented, and the matter is left up to him alone.

However, "One who desires to become pure (that is, to do a mitzvah) is helped." He is not left to battle his evil inclination and the natural preference for inertia

1. Similar to the spies, who concluded that they were unable to go up and conquer the Land of Israel even though they had been commanded by G-d to do so. See *Likkutei Sichot*, vol. 13, p. 40. *Bamidbar Rabbah* 12:3.

2. See *Zohar* II, 162b. See footnote by the Lubavitcher Rebbe in *Sefer Hamaamarim 5703*, p. 12.

3. *Shabbat* 104a. *Yoma* 38b.

alone but is helped and assisted by Hashem to accomplish his good intention, as is understood from the Talmud,[4] which says that **Hashem comes to the aid of anyone who battles to overcome negativity.**

Concerning this, the Talmud provides an analogy:[5] A certain merchant sells naphtha, which has an unpleasant aroma, and also persimmons, which exude a pleasant aroma. When a buyer comes to measure out naphtha, the seller says, "Measure it yourself." But when a buyer comes to measure out persimmons, the seller says, "Wait for me so I can measure it with you, so we can both enjoy the aroma."

Likewise, when we come to do good, before we do it, it may appear a daunting task, but Hashem helps. The only hard thing is just the first step. However, once we "jump in" and start a mitzvah, we are guaranteed that we will then be joined by Hashem, Who stands with us to help us.[6]

This aid, as explained in the *Tanya*[7] is the glow of divine light that Hashem infuses the G-dly soul with so that it may gain strength and superiority over the folly of negativity or the desire for inertia that is often our natural mode unless overcome by a superior light.

THE FIRST STEP

Even though the first step is the hardest, it is the most rewarding because it triggers the ultimate salvation. The Alter Rebbe explains that the beginning of this process is when a person takes the first step by not listening to the voice of the *yetzer hara,* which tries to coax him into giving in to the enticement of indulgence or at least to embrace the natural inclination for inertia. Instead, he empowers his mind over his heart (**"mind over matter"** in common parlance) not to do bad, not even to stagnate, rather, he "jumps in" to do good. This "self-sacrifice" never goes unrewarded—it initiates a guaranteed response from Heaven, and it is at this point that Heavenly help steps in.

---

4. *Kiddushin* 30b.

5. *Yoma* ibid.

6. The splitting of the sea once Nachshon jumped in and the miracles that were performed for Pinchas when he was galvanized to action for Hashem's honor while others dithered attest to the power of this approach.

7. Ch 13, beginning.

When Hashem shines this light on a person, we are able not only to turn away from negativity and inertia, but once we take the first step, new energy comes. Suddenly, what we were trying to accomplish comes together, and with this power, we are able to succeed in a way far more than our natural capabilities and our own merits would normally warrant.

This is true "leverage." With this help from Heaven, it is possible to accomplish great things that under normal circumstances, we may never have thought ourselves capable of.

11

קִדּוּשׁ הַשֵּׁם—לְקַדֵּשׁ (וְלֹא לְחַלֵּל) שֵׁם שָׁמַיִם

Sanctification of Hashem's name—*"Kiddush Hashem"*

The privilege of being chosen as one of Hashem's servants comes with a responsibility—to bring honor, respect, and glory to Hashem through our actions. This is the concept of *Kiddush Hashem.* Therefore, beyond keeping to the "letter" of Hashem's Law through the fulfillment of the *mitzvot* as commanded in the Torah, we should also live with the "spirit" of the law. Everything we do, whether commanded or not, should be in line with Hashem's will—what He would want us to do and how He would want us to do it. Not only does this sanctify everything we do, but also, it brings honor and respect to Hashem.

One of the most significant concepts in our religion is that of *Kiddush Hashem*—sanctifying G-d's Name, which in its simple sense is the requirement under certain circumstances[1] to be prepared even to suffer martyrdom rather than give up our connection to Hashem—a readiness to **sacrifice the body in order to save the soul.** We see historically that when the Jewish soul was demanded, many of our ancestors were ready to give up their bodies to defend it.[2]

Such readiness to sacrifice one's life if necessary, in order to maintain our connection to G-d and not be cut off from Him spiritually, is a sanctification of His name because it shows just how paramount and deep this desire to maintain connection to Hashem is within the soul of a Jew to the point that it is more valuable than life.

There is **an extension of this concept** that we come into contact with daily: the imperative of *Kiddush Hashem*—sanctifying G-d's Name **in daily life**—the desire to maintain connection to Hashem not only by keeping the strict requirements of the **"letter"** of the law but beyond that by keeping and living the **"spirit"** of His law.

Considering oneself responsible for G-d's honor at all times, a Jew seeks opportunities to bring honor (and thus pleasure) to Hashem by "sanctifying His name."

Not only is this so in the eyes of the world, i.e., in public, by behaving in a way that causes others, even

---

1. See *Rambam, Hilchot Yesodei Hatorah* ch. 5.

2. *Kiddush Hashem* has expressed itself historically in the readiness to sanctify G-d's name through martyrdom if necessary. When, as stated above, the Jewish soul was demanded, many of our ancestors gave up their bodies to defend it. The story of Channah and her seven sons is considered to be one of the classic illustrations of such martyrdom.

non-Jews, to praise Hashem, the Torah, and the Jewish people, but, being such an imperative, it applies **even in private** with no one present.

(The defamation of G-d's name—*chillul Hashem*—on the other hand brings disgrace to G-d's name. It is thus a diminution of His honor and considered the most heinous of all sins. Therefore, a person should always be on guard not be the cause of such an occurrence.)

In this spirit, the Talmud says,[3] "The verse 'And you shall love Hashem your G-d' means that the name of Heaven shall come to be loved through you."

One of the classic illustrations of this concept is found in a story as told in the Talmud[4] concerning R. Shimon ben Shetach, a great Talmudic Sage, who dealt in linen to support himself. His students tried to find him a new business because he was exceedingly poor and said to him, "Rebbe, desist from this difficult trade. We will buy you a donkey, and by using it to transport things for others, you will not have to toil so much."

They went and purchased a donkey from an Ishmaelite. The students subsequently found a precious stone dangling from it. The overjoyed students went back to R. Shimon and said to him: "From now on, you need not exert yourself." He asked: "How so?" The students responded: "We purchased a donkey for you from an Ishmaelite, and a precious stone was dangling from it."

R. Shimon asked, "Did the donkey's seller know that the stone was there?" They answered: "No." "In which case," he said, "go return it."

3. *Yoma* 86a.

4. Jerusalem Talmud, *Bava Metzia* 2:5.

The students remonstrated with R. Shimon, "Although theft from an idolater is prohibited, is one not permitted to keep an object that an idolater has lost, as in this case?"

R. Shimon responded, "What do you think, that Shimon ben Shetach is a barbarian, who only thinks about making money? More than all the wealth of the world, Shimon ben Shetach desires to hear people say, 'Blessed is the G-d of the Jews.'"

They returned the precious stone to the Ishmaelite, who was amazed at such honesty and (according to an alternate version of the story) indeed called out, "Blessed is the G-d of the Jews."

What a blessing it is, therefore, for a person to be the catalyst that brings others to praise G-d and his people.

12

"כָּל מַעֲשֶׂיךָ יִהְיוּ לְשֵׁם שָׁמַיִם"

All of one's actions should be for the sake of Heaven

Living in Hashem's presence and being dedicated to His service is an all-encompassing experience. The Torah teaches that everything that we do should be for "the sake of Heaven," whether commanded by the Torah or not, and thereby has the greatest significance—because it is for the ultimate goal of creation—creating a dwelling place for Hashem within this world. In this way, we live for a higher purpose and bring holiness to everything we do.

Everything we do, not just in matters of holiness but even when dealing with the ordinary matters of daily life, such as eating, sleeping, business, and leisure activities, all should be conducted with the intent that they be "for the sake of Heaven"—to fulfill Hashem's will[1] (see section 13a).

In this way, they become holy, and these activities then form part of our service of Hashem.

The Talmud says,[2] "What is a small chapter but upon which all matters of Torah depend?—In all of your ways (even in mundane material matters), know Him."[3]

Therefore, we should ask ourselves and determine before doing something: **"What would Hashem want of me?** Does this act benefit and honor Hashem and His desire to have a dwelling place in this world?"

A person who acts this way, is a true servant of Hashem.

He also draws down upon himself *s'yata di'shmayah*—the help of Heaven in whatever he pursues.[4]

WHY, WHEN, AND HOW

The Torah does not say "no" to permitted material matters; rather, it says "yes," but with a proviso: Before partaking of anything in this world, a person needs to have a clear answer to three questions: "why," "when," and "how," i.e., it has to be for the sake of Heaven and not for self-indulgence (for if not, one becomes "a lowlife with the permission of the Torah"). In keeping with the spirit of this concept, it was the followers of the Alter Rebbe who said that the Alter Rebbe had taught them (see Hayom Yom, 25 Adar II): **"What is is forbidden is forbidden...and what is permitted, one does not need."**

1. This is the concept of **"sanctifying oneself in permitted matters"** (see *Tanya*, chs. 7, 29, and 30; *Overcoming Folly*, Discourse One, Chapter 4, and numerous other sources).

2. *Berachot* 63a (*Avot* 2:12).

3. Proverbs 3:6. See *Likkutei Sichot*, vol. 10, p. 104 and vol. 3, p. 907, where the two expressions "All your deeds should be for the sake of Heaven" and "In all your ways know Him" are explained to be not a double terminology for the same thing, rather two distinct levels in service of Hashem.

4. *Peleh Yoetz* and other sources.

Indeed, the Sages said that by making **His** will (that there be a dwelling place for Him in this world through the use of material things for a higher and holy purpose) to be **your** will, He will then make **your** will to be **His** will.[5]

5. See *Avot* 2:4: "...make His will your will so that He may make your will His will...."

PART TWO

Our Relationship with Ourselves

13a

שִׂמְחָה

Joy

The Torah calls on us to "serve G-d with joy." Joy originates in the mind from the awareness that we are Hashem's chosen servants and thus close to Him. With this one insight, it is possible to see the good, the joy, and the G-dliness within every experience.

A person who believes in Hashem always has reason to be joyous. ***Simchah*—joy—is therefore part of the fabric of life**, especially when focused on the service of Hashem, as King David says in Psalms,[1] *Ivdu et Hashem b'simchah*—"Serve G-d with joy."

Thus, **our concept of joy is unique; it stems from a feeling of closeness to Hashem.** This joy is felt in three ways:

1) **Firstly, the fact that we have merited to be chosen as Hashem's personal servants,[2] entrusted with the task of creating a dwelling place for Him in our world, is the greatest source of joy** (and it is something that G-d Himself derives much joy from[3]).

This is accomplished by studying the Torah and performing His *mitzvot*. Being the will of Hashem, these activities serve to "refine" and "elevate" the world from its mundane, materialistic, and apparently "purposeless" existence. They reveal the true purpose of its creation and in this way fashion a dwelling place for Him here in this world.

In fact, everything we do, even eating, sleeping, conducting business, and engaging in leisure activities, can be part of a person's service of Hashem (see section 12), provided they are done with the proper intention, that is, for the sake of Heaven (as the Mishnah says:[4] "All your actions should be for the sake of Heaven").

---

1. Psalms 100:2.

2. R. Schneur Zalman of Liadi said that a person should feel joy within his soul that he merited to be a servant of Hashem (*Sefer Hamaamarim 5709*, p. 206).

3. *Tanya*, end of ch. 33.

4. *Avot* 2:12.

In this way, a person can indeed fulfill his task and "serve G-d with joy" at all times and in all situations.

GOOD...AND HAPPY

Our traditional Rosh Hashanah greeting for the Jewish New Year: *L'Shanah Tovah Umetukah*—"For a **good** and sweet year," stands in stark contrast to the wish for a "**Happy**" New Year, with which the secular New Year is marked, where the wish is for happiness but without guidance as to how to reach happiness. Our Rosh Hashanah greeting, on the other hand, emphasizes the idea that the best blessing is to see the good in everything, which automatically brings one to happiness.

This ability to be joyous by seeing the good, the joy and ultimately the G-dliness within every experience, was emphasized by the Baal Shem Tov as a primary teaching of the Chasidic way. (Indeed, tradition has it that before the followers of the Baal Shem Tov became known as *Chasidim*, they were called the *freilicher*—the "happy ones.")

Living with this mindset should therefore generate inner joy from our closeness to the King of Kings, the Holy One, blessed is He, having merited to live with Him and to serve Him in His "palace" constantly.

This is what is written:[5] "Israel will rejoice in its maker," that is, any one of Hashem's chosen servants has reason to rejoice in "G-d's joy"—His joy in the dwelling we make for Him in the lower worlds.[6] Since the "upper" and "lower" worlds work in tandem, when a person is *b'simchah*—joyous—in this world, he creates

5. Psalms 149:2.

6. In general, *simchat hachaim*—joy of life—should be a person's guiding life principle, for "joy breaks all boundaries and limitations."

In this vein, it is said that the verse *Ki vesimchah teitzei'u...*—"In joy you will go out...," can be read to mean that "with joy you will go out of all problems and limitations." (This is especially true when praying, which should be done with joy, as the verse says: "These things came upon you because you did not serve Hashem ("service" being prayer) with joy..."). Depression and sadness were always viewed as a dangerous enemy to be kept far away (See *Keter Shem Tov (Hosafot)* §169 where sadness is called a "sin of the Torah." See also *Igrot Kodesh by R. Yosef Yitzchak*, vol. 4, p. 357; vol. 7, p. 196. Depression and sadness damage not only the person himself, but also the channels that bring blessing from Above (*Igrot Kodesh by the Lubavitcher Rebbe*, vol. 4, p. 34, ciing the *Zohar* II, 184b).

joy in the spiritual realms; G-d Himself is, so to speak, also *b'simchah* (and this creates positive channels above for new blessings to reach this world).

2) **Secondly, our closeness to Hashem enables us to speak directly to the King, "face to face," each day, without an intermediary**—an intimacy not granted to others and not even to the "attending angels." This prompted the Sages to establish daily prayers of praise, thanks, and supplications in order to set out for us, as Hashem's personal servants, the language appropriate to use when addressing Him.

THE POWER OF JOY

Whereas it is true that "tears can unlock the gates of Heaven" (*Bava Metzia* 59a), joy, however, has the power to "burst through its very walls" (*Likutei Ramal*—R. Moshe Leib miSasov).

Thus, we say in the prayers, "Joyous are we! How good is our portion...and how beautiful our inheritance": as we would joyously celebrate a large windfall inheritance, all the more so, ad infinitum, should we rejoice over the richness of our inheritance—having been chosen to be servants of Hashem. This is why we should pray with joy (and certainly, a person should banish all sadness from his heart at the time of prayer, and indeed at all times, for sadness and depression are the soul-destroying, sworn enemy of the servant of Hashem[7]).

3) **Thirdly, faith in the divine providence of Hashem also brings joy.** The notion that the Holy One, blessed is He, constantly watches over us and provides all of our needs in magnanimous kindness, like a father concerned over his children, should bring us constant joy, for we have upon Whom to rely: our Father in Heaven who is Omnipotent.

7. See *Igrot Kodesh by R. Yosef Yitzchak*, vol. 4, p. 357 and vol. 7, p. 196.

Thus, joy and happiness in Jewish life come from the feeling of being close to Hashem. It is a state of mind,[8] and this is achieved by appreciating the great merit we have in being servants of Hashem, thus able to pursue G-dly ideals, as explained above.

AS HAPPY AS YOUR THOUGHTS

The *Zohar* notes that the Hebrew word for being "happy"—*b'simchah*—is made up of the same letters exactly as the word *machshavah*—"thought"—a person is as happy as his thoughts are.

Based on the above, King Solomon said,[9] "A happy heart is a constant feast."

8. R. Schneur Zalman teaches in the *Tanya* that our emotions are influenced and fashioned according to our intellect and thoughts. See *Tanya*, ibid (also ch. 26). The *Tzemach Tzedek* once counselled a Chasid to "act as if his heart was full of joy" (even though his heart was not in it), and by doing so, in time, he would become truly happy (*Igrot Kodesh by the Tzemach Tzedek*, p. 323).

9. Proverbs 15:15.

13b

שִׂמְחָה שֶׁל מִצְוָה—שִׂמְחָה הַנּוֹבַעַת מִקִּיּוּם הַמִּצְווֹת

The joy derived from *mitzvot*

Hashem is infinite. Man is finite. Yet, Hashem gave us a way to bridge that gap and connect to Him, by fulfilling His will as expressed in the *mitzvot.* This knowledge is the generator of the joy that can be derived from *mitzvot.*

For a Jew, the joy of "being" is complemented by the joy of "doing." The Torah directive to live life with joy—*simchat hachaim* (as explained in section 13a above), based on the joy inherent in **"being"** a chosen and trusted servant of Hashem, is enhanced and given expression by the **"doing"** part of Jewish life:

Since, as servants of Hashem, we are entrusted with the holy task of keeping the *mitzvot*, it is possible to rejoice in the performance of each *mitzvah*[10] since it is a great merit to fulfill Hashem's will and, in this way, connect to Him. Every *mitzvah* that we have an opportunity to perform is like a gift from the Holy One, blessed is He, connecting us to Him.

If we would bear in mind the infinite greatness of Hashem and, by contrast, the insignificance of man and that despite this seemingly unbridgeable chasm, G-d, out of His great love for the Jewish people, has lowered Himself and given us a way of connecting to Him—by fulfilling His will as expressed through the performance of the *mitzvot*—then we would think of Hashem's *mitzvot* as precious treasures.

This one thought alone can arouse a sense of joy within each person who cherishes the opportunity to serve Hashem through the performance of the *mitzvot* and connect to Him in this way. This is the source of *simchah shel mitzvah*—the joy derived from the gift of the *mitzvot*.[11]

The power of this joy is expressed by the Arizal, who said that the opening of the Heavenly gates of wisdom

10. *Rambam, Hilchot Lulav* 8:15. See *Shabbat* 30b. *Rambam, Hilchot Yesodei Hatorah* 7:4.

11. See *Likkutei Sichot*, vol. 26, p. 211, fn. 18 (*Torat Menachem—Hitvaaduyot*, vol. 54, p. 213).

he experienced and the spirit of divine inspiration he was granted were due to his great joy in performing each *mitzvah*.[12]

12. See *Mishnah Berurah* 669:11.

14

הַכָּרַת הַטּוֹב—לְהוֹקִיר וּלְהַעֲרִיךְ מַעֲשִׂים טוֹבִים

Gratitude and acknowledging goodness

At the core of Jewish character is gratitude for the life Hashem has given us and for the unique connection that we have with Him. Indeed, the word "Jew" originates from *Yehudi*, which comes from *l'hodot*—to give thanks.

The ability to recognize, acknowledge, and be grateful for any kindness done for us is a sign of integrity and good character, while a lack of gratitude reflects the opposite.

We should be especially cognizant and thankful to those who have taught or guided us on the right path in life, for this is one of the greatest kindnesses we can receive, potentially saving us from the pursuit of a wasteful or self-destructive lifestyle.

We learn *hakarat hatov*—gratitude—from Moshe our teacher,[1] who was instructed by G-d to refrain from inflicting plagues on Egypt himself when they involved the Nile River and the earth since they had both once "done him a favor."

Gratitude is an integral part of our life and, indeed, *Yehudi*, the name for a Jew, comes from the verb *l'hodot*, meaning to acknowledge and give thanks—acknowledging the good others may do for us.

However, the greatest expression of gratitude should be directed toward Hashem for all of the kindnesses that He constantly does for us.

As a matter of fact, this was the purpose of the *mitzvah* of *bikkurim*:[2] to bring the first fruits of one's crops to the Temple as a concrete way

FOR EVERY BREATH...

A wise and well-known teaching says: "In happy moments, one should **praise** Hashem. In difficult moments, one should **seek** Hashem. In quiet moments, one should **pray** to Hashem. In painful moments, one should **trust** Hashem. But every moment, one should **thank** Hashem." As the *Midrash* interprets the words of King David at the very end of Psalms (150:6): "Every soul (*neshamah*) praise G-d," the word *neshamah* can be read as *neshimah*—breath—thus interpreting the verse to say: "For every breath, praise G-d." Thus, Psalms concludes with the **"ultimate life lesson"**—gratitude and thanks for the gift of life, this being an essential characteristic of what it means to be a Jew.

---

1. Numerous other examples of our great leaders displaying exemplary gratitude can be found throughout the Torah.

2. See *Sefer Hachinuch, Mitzvah 606*.

of expressing gratitude to Hashem for the gift of sustenance.

Furthermore, on the opening words of the Torah, *Bereishit bara Elokim*—"In the beginning, G-d created," the Midrash intimates that the world was created for the sake of *reishit* (beginning, or first) which is:

(a) the Torah, which is called *reishit* (*first*),

(b) the nation of Israel, which is called *reishit* (*first*), and

(c) the *mitzvah* of *bikkurim*, which is called *reishit* (*first* fruits).

This implies that the purpose of all of the world's creation was just so that people could express gratitude—so fundamental is this to human expression.

The Sages who formulated our prayers were highly sensitive to this insight and gave it reflection in the format of our prayers. It is noteworthy that when the *chazzan* (who leads the prayer services) repeats the *Amidah*, after the congregation has concluded their silent rendition of this prayer, even though the congregation only intone *baruch Hu u'varuch shemoh* after the mention of Hashem's name and *amen* after each blessing in the repetition, the blessings themselves are read aloud by the *chazzan*, who can be an intermediary to petition for our needs.

However, this is not the case with the *Modim* blessing. This prayer expresses gratitude to Hashem for all the great kindnesses that He does for us and is read aloud together by the congregation. One possible reason for this is because **a person should not send someone else in his place to say thank you. When it comes to expressing thanks, we need to do so ourselves.**[3]

Furthermore, if we would reflect on how G-d in His kindness grants us not only life itself but endless good throughout our lives, without measuring whether we deserve the kindness or not, it is possible to feel true thankfulness.

This is the sentiment expressed in the prayer *Nishmat Kol Chai*—"We are not able to thank you, Hashem, our G-d and the G-d of our forefathers, and to bless Your Name, for even one of the thousand myriads of kindnesses, miracles, and wonders You have wrought for us...."[4]

In this vein, just as the Sages established the reading of *Hallel* and *Al Hanissim* for Hashem's many miracles and kindnesses that He did for us as a nation, so should we praise Hashem for the individual kindnesses that He performs for each of us individually in our lives.

Additionally, everyone for whom a miracle is performed and who subsequently praises G-d for it is rewarded with a further miracle, as King David says in Psalms:[5] *Zovei'ach todah...*—"He who offers thanks..." *arenu b'yesha Elokim*—"I will show him the salvation of G-d." **Gratitude brings goodness in its trail.**[6]

---

3. In the name of *Avudraham*.
4. See *Derech Mitzvotecha, Mitzvat Hallel.*
5. Psalms 50:23.
6. This is the theme of the famous *Dayenu* song that is part of the Pesach Seder liturgy: Our acknowledgement and thanks (implied in the expression *Dayenu*) for each small step of the Exodus salvation opened the way for the next and even bigger step of the salvation.

In this vein, we are told about King Hezekiah:[7] "Hashem wanted Hezekiah to be made the *Mashiach*...however, the trait of divine judgment complained to the Holy One, blessed is He, 'Master of the world! If King David, who sang so much praise before You was not made the *Mashiach*, how can Hezekiah, for whom you performed miracles but who did not sing to you, be made the *Mashiach*?'" And this argument was accepted.

So, we see, the redemption has been held up more than two thousand years, since the time of Hezekiah, because he did not express appropriate thanks to Hashem for the great miracles and kindnesses that were performed for him. **This shows just how negative ingratitude can be and how great is the positive power of gratitude.**

7. *Sanhedrin* 94a.

15a

הִסְתַּפְּקוּת

Satisfaction (even with little)

Rare is the human being that says he has "enough." However, the Torah has a recipe for satisfaction: G-d does not bring us into life and then abandon us. He is responsible to provide all of our needs so we may fulfill the purpose for which we were created. Therefore, whatever He gives us must be "enough" for our purpose. It would not make sense for Him to bring us into this world and provide us with less than what we need. Everything we have is therefore a gift to be used for that purpose—a gift...but not ours by entitlement. That realization itself is the greatest gift—that "we deserve nothing...therefore, we have everything."

Satisfaction—that feeling of not lacking anything—is one of life's biggest blessings.

The key to it can be found in one of the basic tenets of the Torah—the stress on the spiritual over the material in order to build "people of spirit." Any preoccupation or overindulgence in material things, more than the sensible measure of what is adequate for a well-balanced life, will diminish a person's spiritual stature, which, ultimately, is the true measure of a person.

Therefore, since Hashem provides all that we need in order to fulfill our purpose in life (which is to serve Him, as explained above) without the need to worry, our ambition in life should be only for things connected to our service of Hashem and certainly not to amass material possessions per se or to satisfy physical drives.

For this reason, it would be both harmful and wrong for a person to strive for and pursue material wealth to a degree more than is necessary for his purpose in life. We ought to be satisfied with a modest proportion of material things (viewing them as adequate to accomplish a person's purpose in life) but strive for more in spiritual matters.

With this mindset, a person is able to live at a totally different level to the rest of society. Society would have us believe that satisfaction, and therefore happiness, come from the accumulation of material possessions. However, the pursuit of wealth, pleasure, or power can never produce the same sense of joy and satisfaction that spiritual pursuits do.

It is man's character that once a certain level of material possessions is achieved, a person wants more of the same and with greater intensity. It is human nature that "he who has one hundred desires two hundred."[1] It follows, then, that as a person desires more, he is less satisfied.

On this theme, our Sages said[2] that when a person leaves this world, he leaves with less than half his desires fulfilled.

The reason behind this phenomenon is that if we were just physical bodies without a soul, then the physical and material gratifications of this world would satisfy us. However, we were created not just as a physical entity—the body and no more.

Rather, as the children of Abraham, Isaac, and Jacob, we have been endowed with a *neshamah*, a soul, and the soul is always going to feel empty from the intake and acquisition of material things because it is by nature not satisfied with material things. So we attempt to assuage this emptiness by further acquisition, which in turn leads to greater "inner" emptiness.

However, **just as the body needs (physical) nourishment, the soul needs (spiritual) nourishment, and this brings "inner" satisfaction**.

Thus, in focusing solely on the acquisition of material things, a person is setting himself up for a life of emptiness and dissatisfaction. (Plus, it's hard to have the "freedom" we think materialism will give us without experiencing its "slavery.")

So, the human experience is that absolute satisfaction can never be achieved in the physical realm—physical pursuits can never lead to true contentment.

---

1. Ecclesiastes 1:34.

2. *Kohelet Rabbah* 1:34 and 3:12.

The Torah path, on the other hand, is the pursuit of spiritual ideals—acknowledging G-d's presence and the G-dliness in life so as to serve Him perfectly and in this way rise to our true potential—this is the true source of contentment and satisfaction because it is the ultimate source of meaning in life.

In the *Aleinu* prayer, which we say three times daily, there is a Torah verse quoted[3] which says: "In the heavens 'above' and on the earth 'below', there is none other...," which alludes to how to achieve satisfaction in life.

The "heavens" alludes to spiritual matters—in these, we must always look "above" to those who have more than us, whereas in the material matters of "earth," we are to look "below" to those who have less.[4] It is not a bad thing, indeed it is positive, to be envious of those who have achieved more **spiritually**, but one should never be envious of those who may have achieved more **materially.**

INNER SATISFACTION FROM MEANING

The paramount value of meaning in life has been attested to in our generation by many a concentration camp and gulag survivor. The willingness to barter meager food rations for the opportunity to perform a mitzvah or some good deed are legion. In one such recorded episode, a son questions his father's decision to use the father's meager ration of margarine as fuel in order to light a primitive Chanukah *menorah* with a strand of thread from his prison garb as a wick. To which the father replied: "My dear son, both of us have unfortunately learned that it is possible for a man to survive one, two, or even three days without food. **But it is impossible to survive even one hour without meaning.**" The message of this story is in line with the oft-quoted insight: "The two most important days in a person's life are the day one is born and the day one finds out why."

3. Deuteronomy 4:39.

4. See *Hayom Yom*, 24 *Cheshvan*.

15b

שָׂמֵחַ בְּחֶלְקוֹ

Rejoicing in one's lot

Everything we receive is designed specifically by Hashem with meticulous and loving care for each of us. This insight enables a person to delight and feel joy with what he has been given.

The two outstanding characteristics outlined above, of *simchah* (joy) and *hakarat hatov* (gratitude), bring in their wake, and create within a person, the most enriching mindset and attitude a person could aspire to acquire in life: **Joy with what one has—*samei'ach b'chelko* (as it says, "Who is rich? He who is happy with his lot").[5] This means not just satisfaction but higher and deeper—actually rejoicing with what we have been given in life.**

Joyfulness, appreciation, and gratitude focus the mind on the good we receive from Hashem and, since He knows our needs, what we receive from Him certainly contains all that we require to fulfill our purpose. **We may not always appear to get what we "want," but we certainly get what we "need."**

THE EXPECTATION

What we are given comes with an expectation: that it be used in a way and for a purpose that helps us fulfill that which we are "needed for."

Hence, the advice[6]: Think less about "what you need" and more about "what you are needed for." Our focus, therefore, should not be on the number of our possessions but rather on what can be done with them.[7]

---

5. *Avot* 4:1.

6. When replying to a Chasid who was saying what he needed, R. Schneur Zalman of Liadi replied that he should think less of what he needed and more about what he was needed **for** (*Sefer Hasichot 5707*, p. 126, where it is further referenced).

7. It is not so much about **what** we get, rather from **Whom** we get it and **why**—it is about the relationship. This idea that we are in a continuous, lifelong relationship with Hashem and that He is involved in everything we do and in everything we have (as explained above at the end of sections 3 and 4) is a fundamental tenet of our belief, which extends to every area of life. Hashem does not just bring us into this world and then leave us to our own devices, as if to say "I have brought you this far, now you are on your own." Rather, He is our lifelong companion, guiding, helping, providing, and teaching as we progress through life so that we can fulfill the purpose that we are "needed for." It is a lifelong relationship.

(The idea that we are in a continuous, lifelong relationship with Hashem, Who guides and helps us through all our issues in life, is expressed in the *Midrash* regarding marriage. When asked what G-d does all day, R. Yosei answered: *Yoshev u'mezaveg zivugim*, literally: He pairs up the married ones. The *Midrash* does not say, as the words could be expected to say, that "He spends His time making *shidduchim*,

This feeling is not limited to those with many possessions, who may find it easy to rejoice in their lot, rather it is within the grasp of every individual, even someone who may have relatively little, since our belief is that Hashem Himself has carefully and lovingly measured to each his lot and thus given each one of us exactly what we truly need in order to fulfill our purpose.

In any case, we see in life that if Hashem wants a person to be successful, he will succeed even if it appears that he has less than someone else. **"Quantity"** is therefore not always the ultimate measure of success. **"Quality"**—finding pleasure with what we are given—is a truer measure of success.

WANTING WHAT WE GET

"If a person is not happy with what they've **got**, they won't be happy with what they **get**."

The main thing is to feel joyous with what we have—as the saying goes: "**The biggest blessing is not so much to get what we want but more importantly that we should want what we get.**"

---

putting together man and woman to make a match." Rather, the literal meaning of the words is: "He joins together the married ones"—those already married. Hashem does not just bring a couple together and then leave them to their own devices. Rather, He is the third partner in every marriage, as the Talmud says (*Kiddushin* 30b): "There are three partners in every marriage: G-d, husband, and wife." He stays with them throughout the marriage as an **active partner**, helping, guiding, and sustaining. So, too, in every area of life, the **key ingredient** is our relationship with Hashem.)

16

זְרִיזוּת, הִתְלַהֲבוּת, וְאוֹמֶץ הַלֵּב בַּעֲבוֹדַת ה'

Energy, enthusiasm, and courage of heart in the service of Hashem

The Torah teaches that all great spiritual achievements begin with one key ingredient: "passion." This breeds the energy, alacrity, and enthusiasm that are the hallmarks of all successful undertakings (and we see in life that this is the case with material matters too).

Passion and zeal—*zerizut*—are crucial to success in anything we undertake in life, especially in spiritual matters.

Indeed, we see that energy and a sense of urgency are the hallmarks of all spiritually attuned people (and one of the consequences of serving G-d joyously), especially as it pertains to the performance of *mitzvot* (as the Sages say:[1] "The energetic are proactive to perform *mitzvot*").

The Alter Rebbe explains[2] that it is only possible to progress in life and overcome the natural inclination for inertia and self-indulgence if one has *zerizut*—a sense of urgency, alacrity, and zeal. He illustrates this with the analogy of two people wrestling. One may be stronger than the other, but if he is lacking *zerizut*, then he will be overcome, even if the one overcoming him is physically weaker. It is the "spirit" that wins.

Warmth and enthusiasm are such powerful ingredients in the service of Hashem that they produce rewards for generations.

We learn this from Abraham—it was the enthusiasm and eagerness with which he went to fulfill G-d's word to bring his son, Isaac, as an offering, that brought merit to the entire Jewish people for generation after generation.[3] This is one of the reasons that it is recalled in our prayer services each Rosh Hashanah.

The vital importance of alacrity in *avodat Hashem* can be seen from one of life's great truths: If we delay the

---

1. *Pesachim* 4a. R. Yosef Yitzchak, sixth Lubavitcher Rebbe said: "The wise act immediately. The foolish delay for tomorrow" (*Sefer Hasichot 5702*, p. 117).

2. *Tanya*, ch. 26.

3. See *Iggeret Hakodesh*, 21.

performance of a *mitzvah*, that opportunity may well not return (and this is true regarding all good opportunities in life).[4]

Either some obstacle may later materialize, or the enticement of the *yetzer hara* (the evil inclination) will be too strong and will cause the *mitzvah* to be delayed, perhaps permanently. (The Sages therefore advised,[5] "When a *mitzvah* comes to your hand, do not let it ferment," i.e., slip by.)

THE STORY OF R. ELAZAR BEN DURDIA

After a life of sin, R. Elazar ben Durdia repented. He did *teshuvah* to the extent that his soul left him as he cried in remorse, and he was welcomed in Heaven as a true penitent. When R. Yehudah Hanassi sensed that R. Elazar ben Durdia had been welcomed in Heaven as a true penitent, Rebbi himself cried and said, "...There is one who acquires his portion in the World to Come in one hour." The question is asked, why did Rebbi cry? Surely, the acceptance of R. Elazar ben Durdia in Heaven as a penitent was a good thing? According to one suggested opinion, the reason why Rebbi cried is because **he was crying for all the others—all of us—** who don't grab the opportunity for repentance when it arrives or those opportunities to accomplish great things (spiritually and also perhaps materially, being all one for a Jew) that come our way in the course of life, which, if not seized upon at that moment, may well be relinquished forever.

This characteristic of *zerizut* is so important that it is alluded to at the very beginning of the *Shulchan Aruch*[6] in the very first passage, which quotes the Mishnah:[7]

"Yehudah ben Teimah says, be bold as a leopard, light as an eagle, swift as a deer, and strong as a lion to do the will of Hashem."

Bold as a leopard: With our individual concerns, we should be humble and willing to compromise. However, with our divine service—Hashem's "concern"—one should be **bold and assertive**, overcoming fear of disapproval, and not be embarrassed by those who mock our service of Hashem.[8]

4. See *Avodah Zarah* 17a, where the story of R. Elazar ben Durdia and his fullhearted embrace of the opportunity to repent came to his hand is recounted.

5. *Mechilta* 21:9.

6. *Shulchan Aruch Harav* (later edition) 1:1.

7. *Avot* 5:20.

8. *Shulchan Aruch Harav* (later edition) 1:1.

Light as an eagle: refers to **energetic enthusiasm** for *mitzvot*.

Quick as a deer: refers to **urgency** in the service of Hashem.

Strong as a lion: refers to the truest form of strength, which is strength and **courage of heart**.

So, the four ingredients necessary for success in *avodat Hashem* are:

1. Assertiveness,
2. Enthusiasm,
3. A sense of urgency,
4. Courage.

All are aspects of the trait of *zerizut*.[9]

However, courage of heart is perhaps one of the greatest attributes. It is the outstanding quality that the Jewish people have exhibited throughout the ages—a steely determination to overcome all hardships in order to maintain our unique Torah way of life. It is the strength to withstand danger, fear, or adversity for the sake of our ideals and what we believe to be true.

This courage of heart creates greatness within a person. With it, we are able to overcome the limitations that crowd in on us, often daily, and we are able to withstand all setbacks in the service of Hashem with a staunch determination. Additionally, it is this courage

9. See *Kitzur Halachot L'Avot u'Banim, Hilchot Tefillah* 4:11, where the alacrity (*zerizut*) of Abraham, when asked by Hashem to bring his son Isaac as an offering, is elucidated. Abraham complied with G-d's command with enthusiastic energy in order to show his joy in being able to fulfill the will of His Maker and bring joy to Him. Our Sages learned from the example of Abraham how we should approach all *mitzvot*. See *Likkutei Sichot*, vol. 4, p. 1319; vol. 10, p. 205; vol. 11, p. 154; vol. 13, p. 289. Above, fn. 2.

that creates the enthusiasm and energy necessary for warm and meaningful *avodat Hashem.*[10]

It follows, then, that a lack of courage is truly one of life's great handicaps.

LOSING EVERYTHING

R. Mendel Futerfas said (paraphrasing a Chasidic saying): "If a person loses his money, he has lost **ten** percent of himself. If a person loses his health, he has lost **fifty** percent of himself. But if he loses his resolve and courage of heart, then he has lost **one hundred** percent of himself."[11]

10. See above, fn. 4. Courage of heart (and fear of Heaven) were one of the characteristics that the Baal Shem Tov was taught the importance of when he was orphaned from his father at a very young age. The last words spoken to him by his holy father before passing were "to fear nothing but Hashem...."

11. See above, section 8, fn. 4.

17

מֹוחַ שַׁלִּיט עַל הַלֵּב

The imperative that the head should rule the heart—“mind over matter”

The key to self-mastery is the power of the head to rule over the heart.

We were all made by Hashem with the innate ability for the head (which is the source of reason and rationality within the person) to rule over the heart (which is the source of impulse and irrationality).[1] G-d designed us with this ability so that we may conduct ourselves according to the dictates of truth and reason.

Nevertheless, we see that this is not always the case; the head does not always rule over the heart.[2] On the contrary, the opposite often occurs.

This happens when there arises from the heart a desire for something, or some act, that goes against either the letter or the spirit of Torah and its values and which, if acted upon, will cause disconnection between the person and Hashem.[3]

When we put aside the imperative of maintaining a connection to Hashem and instead allow the heart and its "whims" to rule over the head and actually cause us to do something against G-d—at that moment, we have been taken over by a "spirit of folly."[4]

This voice or "spirit of folly" is the momentary rationalization that, despite doing something totally antithetical to the will of Hashem, an individual can still be connected to G-d in exactly the same way as before.[5] The "folly" is the rationalization that someone

1. See *Tanya*, chs. 12 and 51.

2. The two opposing forces of rationality and irrationality exist within the person for the exercise of free will.

3. As we see that after Adam's sin, G-d asked him, *Ayekah*—"Where are you?"

4. *Sotah* 3a. See *Tanya*, ch. 19: "...from the *kelipah*, there enters into them a 'spirit of folly,' which leads them to sin, as our Sages remark: 'A person does not sin unless a spirit of folly enters into him.'"

5. *Tanya*, chs. 12, 19, 24, and 25. See *Sefer Hamaamarim 5710*, p. 114 ff. (Besides the actual disconnect from Hashem through sin, submission to the enticement of the spirit of folly places a person in spiritual danger going forward, for he has now granted the *yetzer hara* (in the

can go against G-d and at the same time still be connected to Him.

Indeed, if a person habituates himself to such behavior, our Sages tell us,[6] he falls into the category of "the sinful (and weak-willed), who are controlled by their heart."

The antidote to this is one simple technique—think first.

By having the **presence of mind to think through the consequences** of one's actions, a person will withdraw from doing something that disconnects him from Hashem. (That is why, when the act before him will clearly separate him from Hashem, such as in the case of idolatry, a Jew would even give up his life rather than be separated from Hashem, even for a moment.)

In this way, a person is able to harness the intrinsic power of *mo'ach shalit al halev*—the ability of the head to rule over the heart.[7]

We need to remember that we have the ability to overcome the enticements of the heart as it is within our basic spiritual makeup and our natural ability for the head to rule over the heart. This knowledge empowers a person to withstand, and even more, to overcome and "conquer" the urge to follow the desires of the heart regardless, which is the self-destructive inner drive to hedonism and self-indulgence.

WHO IS STRONG?

Exerting the intrinsic, inner power of the mind to rule over the heart may be the hardest battle, for one is at once the **"victor"** as well as the "**vanquished,**" yet it is by far the most rewarding—granting man dominion over himself. As it says in *Avot*, "Stronger is the one who rules his spirit than the conquerer of a city."

---

guise of this spirit of folly) access to his inner spiritual essence, where it can wreak havoc.)

6. *Bereishit Rabbah* 34:11. See Genesis 8:21. See *Igrot Kodesh by R. Yosef Yitzchak*, vol. 3, pp. 313 -314.

7. See *Tanya*, ch. 12.

"Nature" or "creation" need not be remade in order for us to achieve this. It is intrinsic to our true essence. Knowing this vital fact empowers us to diligently maintain the supremacy of the head over the heart.[8]

This is the key to self-mastery—the hardest earned, but most vital, of all life skills.[9]

THE ALEPH OF CHASIDUT

The story is told concerning the encounter between R. Moshe Meisels (Chasid of the Alter Rebbe) and Napoleon. The event described took place during the Franco-Russian war in 1812, when Napoleon invaded Russia. R. Moshe worked in Napoleon's camp and would pass information to the Alter Rebbe. This information was of use to the Russian army in their fight against Napoleon, to whom the Alter Rebbe was implacably opposed. When attending a meeting of French generals where R. Moshe was present, Napoleon suspected R. Moshe of being a spy and wished to test him. He came up to R. Moshe, put his hand on R. Moshe 's heart, and accused him of being a spy. He wanted to see if R. Moshe's heart would give him away by suddenly fluttering upon being accused. R. Moshe kept his absolute calm, and the incident passed. Later, he told the Chasidim that he had learned the ability to control his heart (which he called the "*aleph* of Chasidut") from the teachings of the Alter Rebbe.

8. See sidebar, where the story is told (from *Igrot Kodesh by R. Yosef Yitzchak*, ibid.) concerning the encounter between R. Moshe Meisels and Napoleon that illustrates this point.

9. The ability to exercise control over our natural drives and instincts is at first a very challenging task. The Talmud (*Berachot* 5a, *Sukkah* 52b, *Kiddushin* 30b) gives practical advice how to prevail against the enticements of the *yetzer hara* in these moments of test. One suggested technique is rather than saying "no," one should say "later," and meanwhile go and do a *mitzvah* ("drag the *yetzer harah* to the house of learning" and study Torah, says the Talmud. Another piece of advice: Yell at him. If that does not work, say the *Shema*. If that does not work, recall the day of death) and in the intervening time, the inclination to sin moves on, for the "fire" has gone and he only works in the "heat" of the moment, before a person can think. That is his sole power. As one continues to wage and win battle after battle, this ability becomes second nature and less difficult (see *Hayom Yom*, 27 Shevat). Furthermore, Hashem does not remain a "debtor" to someone who exerts sincere effort in this struggle, especially if it is waged with *mesirat nefesh*—self-sacrifice.

18

לְכַתְּחִלָּה אַרִיבֶּער—"לִחְיוֹת מֵעַל הַמִּכְשׁוֹלִים"

Living above obstacles (leaping "over" rather than going "under" an obstacle)

The whole attitude and mindset of a Jew should be to live unfazed by challenges, not just when challenges arise but from the outset and all the time it is necessary to live above all the trials and tests we encounter, going right over them.

Rabbi Shmuel, fourth Lubavitcher Rebbe, would say: "The world says that when it is impossible to go under (an obstruction), then you have to go over it. I maintain, however," said the Rebbe, "that in the first place, one should leap over it." That is, one should not be frightened or influenced by challenges and obstacles when it comes to serving Hashem. Don't wrestle with them; go right over them. This is a great principle in life.

An example of this attitude is to be found in a story recorded in the Talmud:[1]

In Temple times, people from all over would ascend to Jerusalem for the three holiday pilgrimages marking Pesach, Shavuot, and Sukkot. On one such occasion, there was no water for the pilgrims to drink due to a prolonged drought.

The Romans had taken for themselves all of the wellsprings that refilled naturally from an aquifer and were thus not dependent on rain, whereas they allotted the Jews only those wells or reservoirs that refilled from rainwater. So when the huge influx of pilgrims arrived in Jerusalem, a very dire situation arose.

One man, Nakdimon ben Gurion, seeing the difficult situation, took matters into his own hands and went to the Roman governor: "Lend me twelve wellsprings of water for the pilgrims to drink from, and I will give you back the twelve wells of water filled with rainwater to compensate in return. If I don't repay you in water, I will give you twelve silver talents" (a huge sum). They

1. *Taanit* 19b.

agreed to a time limit by which Nakdimon would be obligated to pay back the water.

The day came, and the wells had not been refilled by rain. At the time of the morning prayers, the Roman governor sent a demand: "Pay me the water or the money." Nakdimon replied, "I still have time to pay the debt. Water may still fall and fill the wells." In the afternoon, the exchange was repeated. The governor scoffed: "The entire year, rain did not fall, but now in these few moments left in the day, it will rain?" The governor meanwhile went happily to the bathhouse, certain that Nakdimon would need to pay him in silver.

Nakdimon went to the *Beit Hamikdash* and stood in prayer before Hashem: "Master of the universe, it is revealed and known before You that I did not do this for my own honor but for Your honor; in order that water should be available for Your people so they could perform the *mitzvah* of ascending to Jerusalem for the holiday."

The sky immediately filled with clouds, and it rained so much that the twelve wells quickly filled with water. The Roman governor, leaving the bathhouse, met Nakdimon as he was leaving the *Beit Hamikdash*. The governor said, "I know that it is only in your merit that G-d changed the natural order of the world and sent so much rain on the day you needed to pay after a whole year of drought. But it happened too late—the sun set (indicating the end of the day) before it began to rain, so now you must pay me the silver you promised!"

Nakdimon returned to the *Beit Hamikdash* and prayed: "Master of the universe, make known that You have loved ones in Your world." The clouds immediately cleared, and although the time of sunset had passed, the sun could be seen shining—the sun had stood still (as it did for Moshe and Joshua in their time[2]).

The Talmud concludes the story by noting that this is why he was called "Nakdimon," from the word "*nakdah*," meaning "remained," since the sun remained in the sky on his behalf.

From this story, we see that Nakdimon certainly exhibited the sterling qualities of concern for others, trust in G-d, and faith in the power of prayer. However, beyond this, Nakdimon exhibited the one great and unique quality of not calculating the natural likelihood of the wells filling with water (despite the yearlong drought). Rather, since he saw that the pilgrims needed water, he got up and, with the mindset of *Lechatchilah Ariber,* went straight to the Roman governor offering him full wells (or silver) for full wells.

In the end, he merited that not only did rain fall, but a completely supernatural miracle occurred—the suspension of the movement of the sun as Hashem had done for the great leaders of our people, Moshe and Joshua, in their time of need!

From this we see that if a person goes with the mindset of *Lechatchilah Ariber* and remains unfazed by challenges, going right over them, then Hashem will help him with the salvation he needs.

---

2. Ibid. 20a, where it discusses Moshe, Joshua, and Nakdimon as all meriting this outstanding miracle. Jacob experienced a similar miracle—*Vayizrach lo hashemesh*... (Genesis 32:32; see *Rashi* there and *Chullin* 91b) as well as King Hezekiah (II Kings 20:11).

19

הַתְמָדָה

Persistence

Nothing is as soft as a drop of water, and nothing is as hard as rock. Yet, a drop of water is able to pierce the hardest rock...if it hits the rock drop after drop. That's the power of persistence and consistency, the power in life of small but incremental steps taken consistently.

Within each person's soul, Hashem planted many great treasures—powers and abilities that enable us to achieve exceptional things in life.[1]

Among these qualities and characteristics, there is one that is perhaps underrated, yet if a person will harness it, great heights can be scaled in all areas of life, especially in the service of Hashem. That power is *hatmadah*—persistence, diligence, and devotion.

This trait of persistence and consistency is what fuels all personal growth.

Indeed, our Rabbis would often teach that many small actions applied continuously and persistently, one after the other, are more powerful and make a deeper impact than one large, single act.

It is human nature to seek immediate results, but real, lasting change, especially within ourselves, is only achieved with sustained effort.[2]

We find this to be true in the study of Torah specifically, as in the story of R. Akiva and the drops of water upon the rock:[3]

R. Akiva, when still an unlearned shepherd, once saw that small drops of water over time had worn a hole through a rock. R. Akiva's reaction was, "If water, which is soft, can pierce a stone, which is hard, then

1. The verse (Malachi 3:12) that says: "For you (the people of Israel) shall be a desirable land, says G-d" was explained by the Baal Shem Tov to refer to the Jewish soul. Just as the greatest explorers will never uncover the limits of the great and valuable resources which the Almighty has placed within the earth, neither will anyone ever discover the limits of the great treasures which lie buried within the soul of a Jew—G-d's "desirable land."

2. See *Hayom Yom*, 16 *Tevet*.

3. *Avot d'Rabbi Nattan* ch. 6.

words of Torah, which are as solid as iron, will certainly make an impact in my heart of soft flesh."

So, at the age of forty, he went and sat at the feet of a schoolteacher who was teaching Torah to young children. The teacher taught him the *aleph-bet* and he then proceeded from step to step until he had mastered the entire Torah.

The verse thus says,[4] "My Torah will drip like rain." The drops of Torah have the power to penetrate the depths of the heart and brain of every student, as long as he studies continuously and with diligence. This has greater impact than a one-time push of a great deal of learning, in which case its impact is less pronounced and its fruits less far-reaching.

Not only is this principle true in the service of Hashem, but there are many areas of endeavor in life that respond positively to **the power of small but incremental steps taken consistently**.

---

4. Deuteronomy 32:2.

20

מִדַּת הָאֱמֶת

Truthfulness

Hashem is the exemplar of truth. All that He made, He made with truth—it is in the fabric of creation. Therefore, all that we think in our minds, feel in our hearts, speak with our lips, and do with our hands should be true and consistent at all times.

The Torah commands us to be truthful, as it says,[1] *Midvar sheker tirchak*—"Keep away from untruth."

The quality of truthfulness is the most necessary of all character traits and is the foundation to all the others.

Hashem is the exemplar of truth, as it says in the Talmud,[2] "His seal is truth, and He performs truth, and His action is truth," i.e., His trait is truth, and all that He does is truth. Since a Jew is the servant of Hashem[3] and stands in His presence ready to serve Him constantly, as explained above, it is only correct, fitting, and indeed necessary that His servants and attendants should be truthful people.

Additionally, as explained earlier, it is incumbent upon a Jew to resemble Hashem's traits, which includes this essential trait.[4]

Furthermore, truth is vital to the running of the entire world, as our Sages say,[5] "On three things does the world stand: on judgment, truth, and peace." Therefore, we are obligated to accustom ourselves to speak only the truth.

It is written in Psalms[6] that Hashem says, "He who speaks lies will not be established before my eyes." Based on this, the Talmud[7] says that a liar is one of the four types of people who cannot greet the face of Hashem's presence, and their prayers are not heard.

---

1. Exodus 23:7.
2. *Shabbat* 55a and numerous other sources.
3. *Kiddushin* 82a. *Avot* 1:3; *Tanya*, ch. 41.
4. It is said that Chasidim were always careful not only to practice truthfulness between man and his fellow man but also in spiritual matters that pertain to *avodat Hashem*, to be objective and truthful— "not to fool oneself."
5. *Avot* 1:2.
6. Psalms 101:7.
7. *Sanhedrin* 103a.

The Holy One, blessed is He, abhors untruth, to the extent that the Torah says: *Midvar sheker tirchak*—"From a false word distance yourself." Instead of simply saying "Do not lie," the Torah tells us to even "distance" ourselves from untruth. This terminology of "distancing" oneself is not used in reference to any other transgression in the Torah.

Sheker—untruth—is explained as including fabrications of any type, whether in business or personal relationships, including failure to keep promises or even changing minor details when retelling an occurrence.

It follows, then, that since the thoughts of the mind and heart are open and revealed to Hashem and He knows whether a person is speaking truthfully or not, we are obligated to think before speaking in order to carefully weigh and evaluate whether what we intend to say is true.[8]

Furthermore, the Sages tell us that Hashem especially listens to the prayers of those who speak truthfully, as we say three times daily in the prayer of *Ashrei*: "Hashem is close to all who call upon Him"—whomever they are—"to all who call upon Him **in truth**"—as long as they call upon Him in truth.[9]

It could be said that the simple necessity of truth is self-evident and self-understood by every upright

8. There is a saying attributed to R. Zusha of Hanipol: The Torah commands us that *midvar sheker*—from untruth, *tirchak*—keep far away. This can also be read to mean: "*Midvar*" *sheker*—"from" *sheker*, i.e., because of untruth—*tirchak*—you will distance yourself and become far from Hashem.

9. This explanation is according to the *Eitz Yosef* commentary in *Siddur Otzar Hatefillot*. *Radak* explains it to mean that Hashem listens to all those who call to Him in truth—their calls are *emet*. Their calls are determined to be truthful if their words and the intent in their hearts match and are not simply uttering empty words. See *Tanya*, end ch. 37.

person, even without the command in the Torah. However, it is explained[10] that contained within the command to be truthful is an allusion to a deeper notion of truth that the Torah requires of us and without which our service of Hashem is lacking.

Something is only unquestionably true if it is consistent. If something is transitory and changes, dependent upon outside influences, then it is not the ultimate truth. Truth never changes.

We are told, as quoted above, that "The seal of the Holy One, blessed is He, is truth."[2] This is explained to mean that the Hebrew word for "truth"—*emet*—is comprised of the letters *aleph, mem* and *tav*, which are the first, middle, and final letters of the *aleph-bet*.[11] Something is not true unless it is consistent from the beginning through the middle and until the end.[12]

This is in line with what is written:[13] "I am the first and I am the last and aside from Me there is no G-d," meaning that the "truth" of Hashem is expressed in His consistent existence in every place, without change, as is written:[14] "I, Hashem, did not change."

---

10. *Likkutei Sichot*, vol. 31, end of p. 25.

11. Ibid. fn. 2, see *Rashi* commencing with the caption: *Chotamo shel Hakadosh Baruch Hu emet*. The letter מ is the midpoint (the 13th letter of 27— thus having 13 before it and 13 after it) when the final letters מנצפ"ך are included in the count. See *Rashi* on *Shabbat* cited above. (The three letters *shin, kuf, reish* that comprise the word *sheker*—lie—are all next to each other in the *aleph-bet*, indicating that a lie may flow and be easy to say, but their close proximity also means it will have little foundation. The letters *aleph, mem, taf* that comprise the word *emet*—truth—on the other hand are the farthest apart any letters could be in the alphabet: *Aleph* is the first letter of the alphabet, *mem* is in the middle, and the *tav* is at the end, indicating that truth may be difficult to say, but has the strongest foundation. Furthermore, each of the letters that comprise the Hebrew word *sheker* have only one leg, indicating the lack of foundation contained in a lie. Each of the letters of the word *emet*, however, have two legs, indicating the strength of its foundation.)

12. See *Tanya*, end ch. 13.

13. *Isaiah* 44:6; quoted in *Rashi* ibid.

14. *Malachi* 3:6.

Likewise, the true service of Hashem is above change and is unaffected by one's place, one's circumstances, and the object of one's service.[15]

Whether studying Torah, praying, performing *mitzvot*, or utilizing the mundane for the sake of Heaven, either in comfort or hardship, our service must stem from the same consistent and overarching idea: the fulfillment of the will of Hashem. All that matters is the realization of Hashem's will, however that manifests itself, and in this way, we maintain our connection with Hashem under all conditions.

That is the essence of "true" service of Hashem.

TRUTH IS ALWAYS TRUE

An apt illustration of this point can be found in yet another story about R. Mendel Futerfas. R. Mendel was sentenced to imprisonment in the Soviet gulag (forced-labor camps) for the "crime" of organizing and assisting the escape of many Jewish families from Soviet Russia in the dark post-World War II days.

During his time there, he noticed an interesting phenomenon: Within a short period of time of new inmates' arrivals, usually two or three weeks, a large portion of them would succumb to depression. These inmates, many of whom had previously been among the "cream" of Russian society, having been intellectuals, writers, high-ranking army officers, and so on, would wonder how R. Mendel maintained his cheerful and upbeat demeanor, despite the terrible conditions prevalent in the labor camps.

Once, while sitting together, they asked him how he maintained his good spirits.

In response, R. Mendel asked them, "Why is it that you are not happy?" One by one, these new inmates would explain how, prior to their imprisonment in Siberia, they had been in the midst of great projects—one had been writing a book, another was working in medical research, etc. However, now being imprisoned in Siberia, with their life goals having been upended and living in the subhuman conditions prevalent in the camps, they saw no point in going on with life.

"You are all dejected because everything has changed for you—in your life until now, you felt that you were fulfilling some high purpose in your work, but now, this has all stopped. Your imprisonment has prevented you from realizing your life goals," he told them.

"But what about you," they asked R. Mendel, "how come this has not affected you?"

15. See above, section 6, for a fuller elucidation of the teaching of the Baal Shem Tov on this idea that in the service of Hashem, one's circumstances are *shaveh* as in *shiviti Hashem l'negdi tamid*, meaning equal.

"Nothing has changed for me," he said. "I was a Chasid, a servant of Hashem, **before** I came to Siberia, and **now** in Siberia, I am still a Chasid serving Hashem. **My life goal is to serve G-d, and that I can do anywhere**, even in Siberia."

THE TRUTH NEVER CHANGES

The teaching of the Ba'al Shem Tov on the words of King David: *Shiviti Hashem l'negdi tamid* (see section 6) can be applied here. Literally, the words mean, "I have placed Hashem before me constantly." However, the word *shiviti*, being the same terminology as the word *shaveh*, can be implied to mean "equal." When serving Hashem, no matter the *mitzvah* a person is doing, it's all equal since it is an expression of Hashem's will.

21

נֶאֱמָנוּת

Trustworthiness

Hashem brought the creation into being through His speech. Hashem's "word" creates us at every instant, and He does not "go back" on His word. His is trustworthy to grant us life every instant. It is fitting, therefore, that we, His servants, should exhibit the same trait of trustworthiness and keep to what we say.

When a person says that he will do something, it is considered as if he swore an oath. He must therefore stand by his words and fulfill them, as is written:[1] "Guard what comes out of your lips" and "All that leaves your mouth shall you do."

Therefore, before speaking and promising anything, a person must consider whether he will be able to keep his word.

Trustworthiness is so important that the Sages ruled that even someone who says he will give a gift to his fellow and does not give it is *mechusar emunah* (lacking in trustworthiness) and "displeases the spirit of the Sages."

For this reason, when promising something, one should add the phrase *bli neder*—"without a vow, or promise."[2]

A person must also be careful not to change or go back on his word given as an undertaking. This is deduced from the words of the Torah:[3] *hin tzedek yihyeh lachem*—"a truthful measure or scale," referred to in the Torah as a *hin*, "you should use...," which is explained in the Talmud[4] to mean that one's *hin*, which can be read as "yes," should be true, and one's "no" should also be true. That is, when a person says yes or no, he must stand by his decision and fulfill it, especially in matters of business. **A person is not allowed to say one thing and mean another**.

Therefore, a person who regrets and goes back on his word in an already agreed matter of business, even if

1. Deuteronomy 23:24.
2. See *Shulchan Aruch, Yoreh Deah* 203:4.
3. Leviticus 19:36.
4. *Bava Metzia* 49a.

the arrangement was only verbal and no money was yet exchanged, is lacking in trustworthiness and goes against the spirit of the Sages, as mentioned above.[5]

Furthermore, a person who goes back on his word is considered as one who "serves idols" because it exhibits a basic lack of faith. In fact, one of the reasons why the *Kol Nidrei*—the annulment of vows prayer—was instituted on Yom Kippur is to attain forgiveness for those who have not kept their word (which for a Jew is like a vow).[6]

---

5. *Shulchan Aruch Harav, Hilchot Mechirah Umatanah*, 1.

6. The reason for *Hatarat Nedarim* on Erev Rosh Hashanah follows the same logic.

22

קִיּוּם הַהַחְלָטוֹת

Fulfilling personal resolutions

The need for truthfulness extends not only to our interaction with others but even to the "interaction" we have with ourselves—keeping the resolutions and decisions we make with ourselves—"the inner thoughts of our heart"—for Hashem reads the heart.

Truth is not only necessary when interacting with others, but for a Jew, the need for truth extends even to ourselves[1]—we should keep to what we have decided upon in our mind or heart.

Therefore, a person who fears Heaven should keep not only his word but even the "thoughts of his mind," that is, what he has privately decided and resolved to do. This is derived from the verse that says: *v'dover emet bilvavo*—"and he speaks the truth that is in his heart,"[2] for even that which is hidden in a person's heart and mind is revealed and open before Hashem.

For example, if a person thinks and resolves to sell an item to someone at a certain price without informing the buyer of this, he must not then add to the price that he has resolved within himself to sell it at, but rather, he should sell the item at the initial price that he had decided upon in order to fulfill the imperative of *v'dover emet bilvavo*.

A story is told in the Talmud[3] that Rav Safra wanted to sell a certain possession of his. A buyer approached Rav Safra while he was reading the *Shema* and said, "Sell me the object for such-and-such a price." Rav Safra didn't answer since he was in the middle of reciting *Shema*. The buyer thought that Rav Safra was uninterested in the price he had offered, so he increased his offer. When Rav Safra finished praying, he said, "You can take it at the original price you first offered since that was the price I had already agreed in my mind to sell to you at."

---

1. *Bava Batra* 88a. See also *Shulchan Aruch Harav, Hilchot Mechirah Umatanah*, 1.

2. Psalms 15:2.

3. *Makkot* 24a and see *Rashi*, caption: *R. Safra*.

This principle applies not only when selling, but a buyer also should purchase at the original price he decided to pay and not less.[4]

4. *Shulchan Aruch Harav*, ibid.

23

מַעֲבִיר עַל מִדּוֹתָיו

הִתְגַּבְּרוּת עַל הַדַּחַף לִנְקוֹם—

Overcoming the desire for retribution

The person who is able to forgive the slights of others graciously, overcoming the desire for retribution, merits similar forgiveness for himself from Heaven and a "listening ear" above to his prayers.

Our Sages say:[1] "All who humbly overcome the desire for retribution and **forgive insult graciously** are forgiven for all their transgressions."

This is derived from the verse,[2] "Forgiving iniquity and pardoning transgression," which implies: For whom is iniquity forgiven? For those who pardon transgression.

That is, those who forgive and forego the urge for retribution and are imprecise in repaying the harassment of others measure for measure, not responding in anger to those who trouble them, merit in turn that their sins be forgiven in Heaven—measure for measure.

Furthermore, **all doors open for them**. Their prayers are accepted before Hashem, as we see in the Talmud:[3] Once, during a drought, R. Eliezer led a special prayer service on behalf of the congregation and said the twenty-four blessings that were instituted to be said when fasting, but he was not answered.

R. Akiva then went before the ark and said: "Our Father, our King! We have no King besides You! Our Father, our King, for Your sake, pity us!" And it began to rain. The Sages praised R. Akiva over R. Eliezer since R. Akiva's prayer was answered. A Heavenly voice proclaimed: "Not because R. Akiva is greater were his prayers accepted but because R. Akiva is *maavir al midotav*—forgives slight graciously, which was no so with R. Eliezer.

---

1. *Rosh Hashanah* 17a. (See also the notes to *Ein Yaakov Hamevuar*, vol. 6, on *Rosh Hashanah*, p. 90); *Megillah* 28a; *Yoma* 23a.
2. Exodus 34:6–7.
3. *Taanit* 25b.

24

הִתְרַחֲקוּת מֵהַכַּעַס

Keeping away from anger

"Keep far from anger," our Sages advise. Anger is the greatest denial of G-d's providence. When angry, we lose control, and we forget that Hashem is still in control and that He is the source of every occurrence, including the one that is "angering" us.

Anger is a very negative, as well as self-destructive, character trait. Furthermore, our Sages said,[1] "Whoever becomes angry, it is as if they served idols."

The reason for this comparison is because at the time of anger, all of our faith in G-d is lost. The Talmud relates[2] that "a person does not bruise his finger in this world without it being decreed in Heaven, as King David says in Psalms,[3] 'The steps of man are set by Hashem.'" If a person truly believed that whatever was happening to him came from G-d and that this pain inflicted upon him was decreed in Heaven to occur in any case, irrespective of who is causing it (for Hashem has many messengers), then he would not become angry.[4]

Consequently, anger is a complete denial of G-d's providence and is thus like "serving an idol."

For this reason, a person should forego the urge to respond in anger to those who trouble him.[5]

SINAT CHINAM—BASELESS HATRED

The Alter Rebbe explains that one who hates another for the wrong the other did to him is lacking in the faith that Hashem runs everything. The person "causing" the harm is only the messenger from Above to assist the one being hurt in doing *teshuvah*, for there is no *teshuvah* without some pain or discomfort. So this "hatred" is *sinat "chinam"*—it is hatred for nothing.

A story is told about King David[6] that displays his eminence in this regard: While escaping from the

---

1. *Zohar Bereishit* 27b (see *Rambam, Hilchot De'ot* 2:3).

2. *Chulin* 7b.

3. Psalms 37:23.

4. See *Iggeret Hakodesh*, 25. *Likkutei Sichot*, vol. 7, p. 14 ff. *Maamarei Admur Hazaken Haketzarim*, p. 198. See also *Orech Apayim* §1.

5. *Shulchan Aruch Harav* 156:3: "Anger is an extremely bad character trait, stemming from arrogance; therefore one should distance oneself from it to the extreme **and accustom oneself to ignore and not react to the words of those who seek to anger him.**"

6. II Samuel 16:5-13

rebellion of Avshalom, his son, he was met by Shimi ben Geira, who threw dust and stones in King David's face and embarrassed him. Avishai ben Tzruyah, the king's general, requested permission to kill Shimi on the grounds of rebellion against the crown. King David told him to let Shimi be because his embarrassment was decreed from Above: "For Hashem told him, 'Curse David.'"[7]

WHO IS HOLDING THE STICK?

It is pointless to be angry at the stick that strikes, for it is being held by Someone....

Mastering and controlling the tendency to anger can be developed in the following ways:

(a) If a person is being troubled by someone and for this reason falls into anger, he should remember the verse, "I have placed Hashem in front of me constantly." **One is always in the presence of Hashem, and if so, how can he fall into anger?**[8]

(b) With this awareness, that we are in G-d's presence and that it is G-d who is controlling this situation, we should humbly think to ourself: **If I am innocent and undeserving of this difficulty, then I should rejoice, for G-d wishes that I learn the quality of patience and how to accept difficulty and pain with love**[9]**—a most valuable lesson—and this is only a test in order to see whether I will, G-d forbid, lose faith and thus my connection with G-d. And if, on the other hand, I am deserving of this difficulty for whatever reason, I should also rejoice since it is pain sent to cleanse me of my transgressions.**

---

7. Ibid., v. 10.

8. *Igrot Kodesh by the Lubavitche Rebbe*, vol. 18, p. 169.

9. *Gittin* 36b.

(c) If, after all of this contemplation, a person still feels anger rising in his heart, G-d forbid, he should remember what is written in the Talmud[10] on the verse[11] *toleh eretz al blimah*—"He suspends the earth's existence on 'emptiness'": "The world exists because of the one whose mouth is 'empty'—*habolem piv b'shaat merivah*—'one who closes his mouth and refrains from answering at a time of strife.'" **The Talmud is saying that it was worth making the world just for the one who restrains himself from answering back in a time of strife.**[12]

(d) It is worth remembering that **nothing good can ever come from something said or done in anger.**

(e) The Talmud says[13] that there are **three that the Holy One, blessed is He, loves, and one of them is the person who does not become angry.**

We are told that a person who is humble and does not react with anger to those who degrade him will merit that the *Shechinah* will rest upon him and guide him on the right path in life. For this reason, it is said that **before embarking on a new project, one should ask advice from a patient person.**[14]

By implication, one should not ask advice from a person prone to anger, for the Arizal said that when a person is angry, his G-dly soul leaves him. As a result, his *chochmah* disappears, as the Sages tell us: *kol hako'eis*

---

10. *Chulin* 89a.

11. Job 26:7.

12. *Sefer Hamaamarim 5659*, p. 4, quotes the *Reishit Chachmah*, which advises that the best way to overcome anger is to remain silent, not to speak or reply in kind, and this will quieten the desire to respond in anger.

13. *Pesachim* 113b. Furthermore, the Talmud (*Eruvin* 65b) says that a man is recognized in three things, one being his anger—if it overpowers his wisdom.

14. *Orech Apayim* §1, paraphrasing *Orchot Tzaddikim*. (Impatient people tend to look for quick results, which is not always the right solution to every issue. Therefore, they can often "win the battle, but lose the war.")

chochmato mistaleket mimenu—"**An angry person loses his wisdom**."[15] (Plus, says the Arizal, he loses all his *mitzvot* and good deeds[16]—such dire results do not occur with any other transgression.)

It is also written in the Talmud[17] that the students of R. Zeira asked, "How did you attain long life?" To which he responded, "In all my days, I was never angry in my home."

15. *Pesachim* 66b. King Solomon says (Proverbs 19:11): "The wisdom of a person lies in the withholding of his anger."

16. *Orech Apayim* §1.

17. *Megillah* 25a.

25

נְדִיבוּת לֵב

Generosity of spirit and giving way to others

One of the characteristics of a holy soul is generosity. Holiness is complete, and it needs nothing to complete itself; therefore, its nature is to give. An incomplete person, on the other hand, seeks only to take in order to complete himself.

Generosity of spirit (as opposed to strictness and mean-spiritedness) is a beautiful quality that indicates unselfish character and lack of self-centeredness.

Such a person always takes into account the good of another and certainly does not demand aggressively even what is coming to them by rights but rather is willing to compromise and give way in the name of peace and in the spirit of compromise.[1]

The Talmud says[2] that R. Nechunia ben Hakanah merited to live exceptionally long years in the merit of his exemplary *middot*—character traits—one of which was his *vatranut*—his compromising spirit, his willingness to forego the strict measure of what was due to him, especially when it came to matters of money.

This characteristic stems from the inner ability to be happy and feel the joy that comes from giving and sharing with others. Such a person feels no lack when giving of his own to another. On the contrary, he feels complete.

Such people are able to put themselves aside for others.

The Alter Rebbe was once asked: "What is a Chasid?" to which he replied: "A Chasid is one who forgoes his own good in order to do good to another."[3]

This trait mirrors Hashem's way of interacting with us.

Hashem is perfect and complete, lacking nothing, and therefore needs nothing from others—He only gives

1. *See Yoma* 86a. (See *Rambam, Hilchot De'ot* 5:13: "Rather be from the pursued than the pursuers.")

2. *Megillah* 28a.

3. Based on *Niddah* 17a. Quoted in *Igrot Kodesh by R. Yosef Yitzchak*, vol. 8, p. 504. See *Sefer Hasichot Kayitz 5700*, p. 140.

(by creating us continuously). So, too, those who are generous of spirit and whose nature is to be good and strive for holiness also look to give rather than take.

Evil, on the other hand, constantly desires to take since it has no real existence of its own and thus, in essence, is not complete; it needs to receive from others in order to be whole. An uncompromising and ungiving spirit thus indicates selfishness and self-centeredness—the opposite of holiness.[4]

GIVERS AND TAKERS

"Takers" see themselves at the center of the universe, around which everything else revolves, including G-d. "Givers," on the other hand, feel that it is G-d Who is at the center of everything, and it is they who revolve around Him.

This explains why Eliezer, the servant of Abraham, when searching for a match for Abraham's son Isaac, chose to test Rebecca's suitability with *chesed* (lovingkindness).[5] Although it is true that *chesed* was a hallmark of Avraham's household, nevertheless, there were many other sterling characteristics that would have indicated her suitability, such as adherence to Torah, *mitzvot*, modesty, and prayer, all part of living a life built on holiness. Why did he choose *chesed* to be his determining factor?

Eliezer understood that *chesed*—giving to others and a lack of self-centeredness, i.e., **giving rather than**

---

4. *See Tanya*, ch. 19: "...the side of holiness and humility stands in direct contrast to the side of *kelipah* and *sitra achara*, which acts only for itself and says, 'Give, give...feed me,' because they are separate from G-d," whereas the side of holiness wishes only to give.

The Rebbe explains (*Likkutei Sichot*, vol. 25, p. 80) that there are two types of *chesed* giving—the *chesed* of Ishmael, where the giver gives because of the grandiose and proud view he has of himself, giving "leftovers" to others but keeping the main part for himself. Then there is the *chesed* of Abraham, which comes from *bitul*—humility, feeling that others are more important than oneself, and in this way, he is prepared to give the main part of what he has to others while keeping the "leftovers" for himself. Such people are able to put themselves aside for others.

5. See Kehot Chumash *Bereishit*, which quotes this explanation of the Rebbe on the verse (Genesis 24:14): "...and also to your camels I will give to drink."

taking—is the ultimate expression of holiness and would be the key indicator whether Rivkah possessed a holy soul fitting to join Abraham's family.

26

עֲנָוָה—צְנִיעוּת וְהֶעְדֵּר יֵשׁוּת עַצְמִית

Humility and self-effacement

Hashem is infinite. Before Him all is as nothing. Yet He is humble—He contracts His infinity in order to interact with us. So it is fitting for each of us to exhibit the same trait, as do those who are truly great. Arrogance is therefore foolish, as well as unbecoming.

One of the hallmarks of insightful and connected people is the awareness that we are constantly in Hashem's presence, as is written:[1] "I have placed Hashem before me constantly," and that in actuality, nothing truly exists other than Hashem, including the person himself, as is written:[2] "There is nothing other than Him." This recollection arouses within the person **a sense of humility**, a character trait that is fundamental to all truthful service of Hashem.

It is also the **key to success** in many areas of life, especially interpersonal issues, fostering good grace, the ability to handle the "trials" as well as the "triumphs" of life with equanimity, keeping one from anger, quarrelsomeness, coveting what others have, feelings of revenge or grudge, and sadness. It helps one see good in others and to experience the the joy of giving. It cultivates satisfaction with one's lot, keeps one from jealousy, and cultivates gratitude and joy for every blessing and every opportunity. It helps develop the ability to truly empathize and feel the need of another and opens one to accepting positive criticism and internalizing the hard-earned but valuable lessons of life we come across from time to time during the course of life.

Humility is therefore a fundamental value to aspire to in life, being the key to many other values, and brings with it much blessing.

Arrogance, on the other hand, is a very negative quality (as is written:[3] "An abomination to Hashem is the proud of heart," and the Sages say,[4] "Concerning one

1. Psalms 16:8.

2. Deuteronomy 4:35.

3. Proverbs 16:5.

4. *Mishnah Sotah* 5:1; *Avot* 4:4. (See *Tamid* 32a: "What should a person do to live? *Yamit et atzmo*—"He should kill himself," and *Rashi* explains the term *yamit* ("kill") to mean *yash-*

with a haughty spirit, G-d says, 'He and I cannot dwell together in the world'"), and it is forbidden even in the smallest degree.[5] It is the source of many, if not most, character defects and, furthermore, is senseless.

We are instructed that a person should accustom himself to be humble, as the Sages directed:[6] "Very, very much, be of low spirit" and "Be of low spirit before every man."[7] True humility is the *bitul*—lack of "self"—that comes from an awareness of Hashem's presence,[8] as mentioned above.

We learn humility from Moshe, our teacher, who, despite his spiritual stature,[9] was "more humble than any man"[10] since he felt insignificant before the infinite Holy One, blessed is He, the only true existence. Thus, he knew that all of his lofty qualities were given to him by Hashem[11] and were not his own doing. He felt that if his capabilities would have been given to others, they too could have

THE GREATEST ARE HUMBLE

Chasidim would say that the job of a person is to make from אני ("I") into אין ("nothing"). Both words contain the same letters. It is only necessary to rearrange them in a different order.

---

pil—**humble** himself.) If a person is caused pain by another, the fitting reaction is not anger because, after all, it was Hashem who brought about the situation whereby the other person would be the cause of this pain. In general, it is always better to be humbled than honored. If anything, one should feel sadness that one's friend is sinning by causing this pain, which thereby causes pain and "blemish" Above.

5. *Rambam Hilchot, De'ot* 2:3.

6. *Avot* 4:10. See *Likkutei Sichot*, vol. 4, p. 1212.

7. See *Likkutei Sichot*, vol. 13, p. 30; vol. 17, p. 1.

8. Furthermore, Hashem's presence will only rest on something that is *battel*—nullified—to Him (*Tanya*, ch. 6). See *Derech Mitzvotecha* 62a. See *Sefer Hasichot 5700*, p. 140, where a Chasid is defined (along with other sterling character traits) as one who views others, even the most simple, as being better than himself.

9. As evidenced by the fact that he was not only chosen to take the Children of Israel out of Egypt, but Hashem promised him that "they will believe in you forever." Furthermore, he could speak to Hashem at all times, he received the Torah for us from Hashem, and he was taught the Torah directly by Hashem on Mount Sinai for forty days. Many other instances abound of Moshe's greatness.

10. Numbers 12:3.

11. *Likkutei Sichot* cited above, fn. 6.

attained his stature—or an even greater stature—and he was thus humble before all men.

The ultimate paradigm of humility is Hashem. Despite His infinite loftiness, He "lowers" Himself, so to speak, to be concerned with our affairs in this limited and temporal world. Thus, by cultivating the trait of humility, we are able to emulate Hashem and go in His ways.[12]

The Baal Shem Tov taught that even though we should cultivate the trait of humility within ourselves, nevertheless, when it comes to another Jew, we should only see his greatness and spiritual grandeur.

12. Humility is one of the three components of the general characteristic of modesty—*tzniut*. The other two are privacy and holiness. Hashem exhibits these three characteristics of humility, hiddenness, and holiness. Thus, by being humble, preferring hiddenness to visibility and publicity, and aspiring to holiness, we emulate Hashem.

27

הַכָּרַת עַצְמוֹ

Recognizing one's own qualities

There is one area of knowledge in life that is extremely valuable, and without it, one can accomplish little. However, with it, everything is possible, and that is to know ourselves—our weaknesses and our strengths, especially our greatest strength, which is the soul we have been given and its awesome powers, for with that knowledge, everything is possible.

Truthfulness, especially in the service of Hashem, requires us to know ourselves—both our flaws and our virtues.[1]

It is important to know one's flaws in order to repair them and one's virtues in order to know one's capabilities and what one can therefore demand from oneself (and consequently, a person will have no excuses for failing to live up to their potential).[2]

The ultimate virtue that each person possesses is the gift of the soul. Indeed, Chasidic teaching stresses the inherent greatness of every Jew, each one of us being the recipient of an infinite G-dly soul,[3] which is literally a part of G-d Himself.

KNOWING WHO YOU ARE AND WHO YOU ARE NOT

R. Zusha of Hanipol is famously quoted as having said: "After my time in this world, I am not worried that they will ask me in Heaven: 'Why were you not like Moses?' Rather, I am worried that they will ask me: 'Why were you not like Zusha?'"

Within the soul have been placed immense powers and abilities. With these, it is able to outlast everything and overcome all obstacles, never losing its intrinsic connection to G-d while here in this world, where it has been sent from

1. *Sefer Hasichot 5687*, p. 114. *Hayom Yom*, 21 Adar I and 26 Cheshvan. *Likkutei Diburim*, vol. 3, p. 430; vol. 4, p. 581. "There are those who have a tendency to think only negatively of themselves. This is 'nonsensical humility'—a trap that can destroy a person" (*Igrot Kodesh by R. Yosef Yitzchak*, p. 63). Besides the demands of truthfulness that require an honest and realistic understanding of oneself, in general, one of the fundamental requirements for success in both material as well as spiritual matters is objectivity, and the lack of it can prove to be a great handicap in life. Many people go through most of life as complete strangers to themselves.

2. Awareness of one's good qualities, nevertheless, should not cause *gaavah*—haughtiness—or pride since the innate talents a person is blessed with are a gift from Above (see above, section 26). See *Likkutei Sichot*, vol. 13, p. 30 (and the sources listed in fn. 7); p. 37 (and the footnotes there). Also, vol. 17, p. 4, where the humility of Moshe—"being the most humble of all men"—is elucidated.

3. Job 31:2. See Psalms 16:5 and 73:26. Jeremiah 10:16. See *Tanya*, beginning ch. 2. See *Likkutei Sichot*, vol. 4, p. 1202, on *Avot* 3:1.

its G-dly source in order to accomplish a mission (that it could not achieve while in its source Above).[4]

Living with this awareness of our inherent greatness and spiritual grandeur can empower us to rise above all tests and challenges in life, for, in this way, even though a person lives within this world, nevertheless, he remains connected to Heaven, as R. Meir of Premishlan said: "When you are connected Above, you don't fall down below,"[5] and we are indeed able to live up to our potential.

KNOW YOURSELF

"No one can stop you if you believe in yourself, and no one can help you if you don't."

4. See *Torat Menachem—Sefer Hamaamarim Melukat*, vol. 1, pp. 246-249, (in English: *The Unbreakable Soul* (Kehot, 2001). There, the Lubavitcher Rebbe explains that G-d desires for the soul to experience the most intense form of Divine service, that of the *baal teshuvah* (one who "returns"—even when not spurred by having sinned—but rather the soul's desire to "return" to its source), which is greater than the service of *tzaddikim*, what the soul experiences in its source Above. This is borne out by the saying of the Sages (*Avot* 4:17): "One hour of repentance and good deeds in this world is worth more than all of the life of the World to Come," and as the Talmud says (*Berachot* 34b), "In the place that *baalei teshuvah* stand, perfect *tzaddikim* cannot stand." In line with this teaching is the saying: "A Jew is not a physical being who sometimes goes through a spiritual interlude. Rather, a Jew is an everlasting G-dly and spiritual being who is going through a physical interlude—its sojourn in this world."

5. *Torat Menachem—Reshimat Hayoman*, p. 265; *Sefer Hasichot 5696*, p. 95 ff.

28

עֲשֵׂה לְךָ רַב—הַצֹּרֶךְ בְּמוֹרֶה־ דֶּרֶךְ וּמַשְׁפִּיעַ בַּחַיִּים

The need in life for a guide and mentor

“Love is blind”...self-love especially so. This can “blind us” to the reality of our own issues. Lack of objectivity can lead to poor decisions in life. A “blind” person needs a guide, so our Sages advised us to find that guide—a trusted and objective mentor, someone wise who has our interests at heart. Such a mentor is a precious resource to have in life.

The Sages understood the psychology of people. Because we are by nature not always objective when it comes to personal matters, they therefore advised everyone to seek out a mentor and guide to discuss important issues with and thereby gain that extra dimension of objectivity that is so necessary in making successful decisions.

Thus, it is written in *Pirkei Avot* (not once but twice):[1] *asei lecha rav*—"Make (provide) for yourself a teacher."

The Lubavitcher Rebbe taught that every individual should look for and accept upon themselves a *mashpia*, a mentor, from whom to seek and receive advice in the service of Hashem because "man is close to himself" and cannot depend upon his own self-evaluation.

RISING ABOVE ONESELF TO SEE THE SITUATION AS IT LOOKS FROM ABOVE

A person involved in his own decisions cannot always answer objectively the key question: How does G-d see this situation? What would G-d expect of me in this situation? A mentor who is knowledgeable in the Torah way of thinking can help a person arrive at a decision based on what G-d wants rather than merely what the person desires.

This mentor will guide a person correctly in the ways of Torah, Chasidut, and good sense, so that a person can avoid the fear that his judgment of an issue might be tainted by "self-love."[2]

R. DovBer, second Lubavitcher Rebbe, taught that when one Jew asks another for advice, **two G-dly souls** are pitted against **one animal soul**. Although the person whom you are asking also has an animal soul, his animal soul is not at all concerned with the desires

1. *Avot* 1:6 and 1:16.

2. See *Shulchan Menachem*, vol. 4, p. 185 ff., in reference to *asei lecha rav* (also the references in *Sefer Hamaftechot Lesichot Kodesh*, p. 671, under the heading *Mashpia*).

of his colleague, whereas the G-dly soul of one cares about the G-dly soul of the other.[3]

3. *Hayom Yom*, 20 Tevet. See also there, 25 Sivan, where the advice of the Talmud to "talk over one's worries with another" is quoted and explained with an insight of the *Tzemach Tzedek* who said that the "others" the Talmud refers, to are only "others" in the bodily sense. However, in heart and spirit, they are not "others," for they are completely united with him since they empathize with him.

29

יֹקֶר הַזְּמַן

Appreciating the value of time

Every day, every hour, every minute, and every breath is a precious gift. None of it is ours by right or entitlement. It was given only so we may achieve the great deeds and triumphs for which we are granted the gift of time.

Time is one of the most precious gifts (besides one's good health) given to us by Hashem. In fact, the first commandment given to the Jewish people as a nation related to time.[1]

Each individual is given a limited amount of time that cannot be reused, and a person who wastes even a moment of their life has, for that moment, "taken their own life," so to speak, since every moment is an integral and important part of life, and a wasted moment can never be reused. As such, wasting time is the greatest misuse and greatest waste possible in the life of man.[2]

A person needs to remember that tomorrow is promised to no one.

Therefore, it is necessary to appreciate and treasure the gift of time. This is especially so while a person is still young, when the heart and mind are open to the learning of Torah and the service of Hashem.

This is hinted to in the verse:[3] "How will I go up to my father, and the youth is not with me?" For each person has to ask himself, "How will I go up to my Father in Heaven at the end of my days, and the days of my youth are not with me because they were wasted?"

Rather a person should watch over his youthful years especially, that they not be wasted and swallowed up in matters of little or no value.

---

1. This was the command to establish a calendar. See Exodus 12:2. See *Rashi's* comment on 12:2.

2. This is in line with the explanation given on the verse (Genesis 24:1): "And Abraham was old and came (i.e., was full) with his days," implying that he came with all his days since not a single one went to waste. Rather, he had used each one constructively for the service of Hashem so that each one counted.

3. Genesis 44:34.

However, should a person come to this realization only later on in life, all is not lost. By taking action, one can still save something—it may not make for us a better "beginning," but it can, however, make for us a better "ending."[4]

There is a well-known saying:[5] "Man worries over the loss of his money but does not worry over the loss of his days; his money returns, but his days do not return." And it's the days that count. For even though our "years" cannot be lengthened (the number of years we are allotted in life), our "days" can be lengthened by filling them with things of eternal value.

THE YEARS FLY BY, BUT A DAY CAN LAST FOREVER

This is encapsulated in the oft-quoted saying: "Today may not come around again, but one good deed can make it last forever."

Consequently, a person should try to use and "rescue" every free moment for things of enduring spiritual value—Torah, *mitzvot*, and the service of Hashem.

In one of their teachings,[6] our Sages provide practical advice on how to accomplish this ideal and achieve optimum use of our time by prioritizing what we spend it on: "Whoever takes upon himself the 'yoke' of Torah, the 'yoke' of worldly cares and worries will be removed from him; but whoever casts off the 'yoke' of Torah, then the 'yoke' of worldly cares and worries will be imposed on him."

Every person has a "yoke" to carry in life. However, we get to choose it. If a person wishes, the "yoke" can be

4. See *Avodah Zarah* 19b. *Rambam, Hilchot Teshuvah* 2:1.

5. *Sefer Hachaim* (by the brother of *Maharal* of Prague).

6. *Avot* 3:5.

Torah, in which case Heaven will remove the "yoke" of worldly cares.

Conversely, if a person wishes to carry the "yoke" of worldly cares, then he will have no time for Torah and matters of enduring value. **So what we get out of time is entirely up to us.**

30

שְׁמִירָה מִפְּנֵי סַכָּנָה רוּחָנִית

Avoiding spiritual danger

Spiritual danger can wreak as much havoc as physical danger. One needs to take both seriously.

From the Torah's perspective, the body and soul of a Jew are equally precious, being that they are both vital for the service of Hashem. Therefore, just as it is forbidden to place oneself in physical danger (as explained in section 52), **so too is it forbidden to place oneself or others in spiritual danger—a situation where one could come to do something that is against G-d's will and, by extension, one's own true good.**

A person who lives with the awareness that he is always in the presence of the Almighty is living a life connected to Heaven. For this reason, he will always maintain an element of diligence, that he not do something that could sever this precious connection. He is "fearful" of becoming disconnected from the Heavenly source of life Above.

Therefore, *Yirat Shamayim*—literally "Awe of Heaven"—is at the root of King David's directive in life:[1] "Turn away from (something that could bring you to) evil (in order to) do good."

It is not enough to serve Hashem with "love" alone; rather, we must awaken the natural "fear" of G-d that is hidden in the heart of every Jew—the "fear" of being disconnected from Hashem, which would come about by doing something that is against His will.[2] This is called "fear of sin"—a person is fearful of doing something against Hashem's will because doing so triggers a disconnection between the person and Hashem.

THE KEYS

R. Shalom DovBer, fifth Lubavitcher Rebbe, said that the keys to the Heavenly chambers above are given to those who serve Hashem with *kabbalat ol* (acceptance of the yoke of Heaven) and with the sincerity of *yirat Shamayim* (awe of Heaven). These are the keys that unlock all the doors above (*Igrot Kodesh by R. Yosef Yitchak*, vol. 6, p. 272).

---

1. Psalms 34:15 (see *Sefer B'shem Omro* on this verse).

2. *Tanya*, beginning of ch. 41.

Indeed, it is explained[3] that fear of sin is actually fear of what sin is in essence—disconnection (from Hashem), for the word for sin in hebrew—*chet*—is from the same terminology as *chesaron*—which means lacking in connection to Hashem.

For this reason, the Sages advised us[4] to erect safeguards, "fences" and barriers ("no-go" areas), around sins—those particular issues in which we may be prone to stumble and in this way help keep us far from actual transgression.

In this way, a person can be "on guard" to avoid allowing himself to be drawn into situations that may start innocently enough but will, like the "thin end of the wedge," end in sin ("for such is the way of the *yetzer hara*, today he says 'do this' (which could be something quite small and seemingly 'inconsequential' initially), and tomorrow (i.e., once habituated to listening to the *yetzer hara*) he says 'do that' (something worse)...").[5] Then, as our Sages tell us,[6] a downward spiral begins, for just as one good deed brings in its trail another good deed (*mitzvah goreret mitzvah*) so too does one sin bring in its trail another sin (*aveirah goreret aveirah*).[7]

THE HANDLE

Creating a "fence" to distance oneself from undesirable practices also requires "help from Heaven," and we therefore pray for this each morning when we ask Hashem: "Do not bring us ***lidei*** *chet*—literally "to the "**hand** (or **handle**) of sin," when it should really have said "do not bring us to sin." Everything has a handle by which one gets ahold of the thing. Sin also has a handle. First comes the handle—a person starts not by sinning but by just holding the handle, i.e., he gets near to the sin, which is rationalized with the thought, "I am not actually sinning, I'm just getting near." Then it is just a tiny step to do the sin, which is rationalized with the thought, "I was near the sin before and nothing happened, so actually doing the sin now is not much different from before when I was just near it." However, if a person creates a fence in front of the sin, the fence stands in the place of the handle, keeping the sin far away.

3. *Likkutei Sichot*, vol. 4, p. 1200 (and the sources cited there).

4. See *Avot* 1:1.

5. *Shabbat* 105b. *Niddah* 13b.

6. *Avot* 4:2. See *Likkutei Sichot*, vol. 20, p. 355.

7. Based on this principle, we are told that if a person is unsure whether what he just did is really good, i.e., a *mitzvah*, or not, he should

So, to avoid such a scenario, King David advised us to actually "turn away" from spiritual danger in the first place.[8]

(The greatest spiritual harm can come from opening oneself up to everything that one sees, granting unchecked and unfettered access for all the spiritually harmful stimuli that abound in the outside world.

Each person thus has an obligation to bolster their defenses against spiritually harmful influences and situations, and one of the main tactics in this effort is control of one's eyes[9] by averting them when necessary from gazing at inappropriate things, as is explained in section 55.)

---

think back to what he did just prior to that. If it was something good—a *mitzvah*—then the next thing is also a *mitzvah*. If, however, it was not good—an *aveirah*—then the next thing is also an *aveirah*.

8. See the explanation of the Sages in *Avodah Zarah* 18b on the first verse of Psalms, which is explained to allude to this chain of negative causality.

9. See *Avodah Zarah* 20a: "'Be on guard (and turn away) from evil'—a person should maintain a guard on his vision in order to avoid seeing inappropriate things...."

31

שְׁמִירַת הַבְּרִיאוּת

Guarding one's health

Good health is a precious gift from Hashem to be appreciated and not to be taken for granted. The Torah therefore instructs us to protect it as one would protect a priceless treasure.

It is a *mitzvah*, a command of the Torah, to conduct ourselves in a way that will help preserve and optimize our natural good health (which is a precious gift from G-d), as the verse says: "Guard yourself and guard your soul very carefully,"[1] for a person cannot serve Hashem properly if he is, G-d forbid, weak or ill.[2] Therefore, a healthy and whole body is part of serving G-d.[3]

The saying of the Maggid of Mezritch is well known:[4] "A small hole in the body is a large hole in the soul."

(Details of the regimen that is considered to promote good health (based largely on the writings of Rambam), are cited in the *Kitzur Shulchan Aruch*, and a brief synopsis follows:)

One should eat foods that contribute to good health (and part of one's diet should contain foods such as fruits, vegetables, and other natural foods that are recognized for their nutritional value), and one should refrain from consuming unhealthy foods.

Digestion commences in the mouth, even before food reaches the stomach. As such, many illnesses that are attributed to poor digestion can be the result of improper chewing and inadequate mixing of the food with saliva. Taking the time to chew correctly is important for good health.

A person should not eat until total satiation, for if the stomach becomes full, digestion is more difficult

---

1. Deuteronomy 4:9-10. See *Shulchan Aruch Harav, Hilchot Shemirat Guf Venefesh*, for various laws in this regard.

2. Ibid., *Orach Chaim* 155:1. (See *Hilchot Shemirat Haguf* in *Kitzur Halachot l'Avot u'Banim*).

3. *Rambam, Hilchot De'ot* 4:1.

4. Part of a letter written by the Maggid to his son, quoted in *Likkutei Sichot*, vol. 10, p. 4. See *Hatamim*, Issue 7, p. 28 [664].

because the stomach cannot expand and contract as it should in order to break down the food. Rather, a person should eat only as much as is necessary in order to satisfy his need (this is about ¾ of one's fill). A technique some use is to plan initially before eating to eat only around ¾ of the food on the plate. (In general, if one looks upon food more as "fuel" for the body and less as a source of pleasure,[5] then it is possible in this way to master the "hold" that food can exert on our psychology.)

Not only is the quantity of food a person eats of importance, but equally significant is the time of the day that one eats. (There is a common saying that in the morning, one should eat like a king, in the afternoon like a prince, and in the evening like a pauper. Sumptuous eating before bedtime is not good for the health.)

Eating bread, or at least a solid meal in the morning, contributes to good health.[6]

Water is a natural beverage that is most suited for the body. One should drink water periodically throughout the day and preferably before eating rather than in the midst of the meal. Drinking water keeps the body well hydrated and aids prompt elimination.

Exercise in moderation contributes to good health, and it is best either to walk or to exercise before eating

---

5. The Sage Hillel, when going to eat, would say that he was "going to perform an act of kindness with his lowly body." He was at the rarified level where the soul was his true identity and not the body. To him, the body felt like a separate entity and subsidiary to his true essence—the soul. Despite his exalted status, his comment nevertheless contains a lesson, to one degree or another, for everyone. See *Tanya*, ch. 29, quoting *Shemot Rabbah* 34:3.

6. See *Bava Metzia* 107b, where several advantages of such behavior are enumerated. (See *Rashi* on Genesis 18:5 on the words: *vesaadu libchem*—"that you may nourish your heart"... bread is the nourishment of the heart, i.e., it is thoroughly satisfying in general.)

rather than afterward. The Torah states, "By the sweat of your brow, you shall eat bread," and King Solomon wrote, "She...does not eat the bread of idleness."[7]

It is important to maintain regularity each day, in keeping with the natural function of the body which is able to separate the food we ingest into that which is needed and that which is not needed. It does this by absorbing food until it becomes part of the body, sending the good nutrients within the food to their destination, down to the microscopic and cell level, and then rejecting what is not needed or is harmful to the body. Eliminating what is unwanted by the body with daily regularity is a key factor in maintaining good health, and delaying the natural urge to do so can, G-d forbid, lead to illness.

This process, namely, to be able to absorb and assimilate food, which is something "foreign" and external to the body, to the extent that it actually becomes part of us—retaining that which is nutritious and then rejecting that which the body cannot benefit from—exhibits exquisite wisdom and is the trigger for the unique blessing we recite for the wondrous workings of the body, known as the blessing *Asher Yatzar*.

It is said in the name of Rambam that the key to good health is hinted at in the 6 letters of the Hebrew word "ב'ר'י'א'ו'ת"—"*briut*," meaning health, which stand for ***B****olea* ***R****ogzo* ('ב'ר), ***Y****am'it* ***O****chlo* ('י'א), ***V****eyarbeh* ***T****enuos-av* ('ו'ת)

B*olea* ***R****ogzo* (lit. swallow, subdue your anger)—Keep away from anger and emotional stress. Rather, a

---

7. Proverbs 31:27.

person should accustom himself to positive traits like joy, calmness, being content at all times and in all circumstances, humility and so on. Traits like worry, fear, stress, tension, and anger are harmful to one's life (not only to the body, but to the soul also).

Take care not to eat when angry, fearful, or anxious (as the body releases toxins at such moments). Rather, one should be in a serene and moderately happy state of mind when eating.

***Y**am'it **O**chlo* (lit. limit one's food intake)—A person should accustom himself to eating slightly less than he desires to eat (ideally no more than ¾ of what he desires, as mentioned above) and one should always leave over some food on the plate. This is dignified and healthier. (The Talmud says, "A meal you enjoy, abbreviate it").

***V**eyarbeh **T**enuosav* (lit. be increasingly active)—It is good for one to exercise and exert effort by walking or working, especially before sitting down to eat. This is alluded to in the verses, "By the sweat of your brow shall you eat bread," and "(she) does not eat bread of idleness").

PART THREE

Our Relationship with Others

32a

אַהֲבַת יִשְׂרָאֵל

Love for a fellow Jew

Ahavat Yisrael—love of every Jew is the central principle of the Torah. It is a love based on what we all have in common—the soul. Even though the body may separate us, it is the soul that unites us, for each of us is part of one G-d, Who is the Father of us all.

The Torah commands that we love every Jew as we love ourselves (as the verse states,[1] "And you shall love your fellow as yourself").

R. Akiva said that this commandment is a great principle of the Torah.[1] Hillel the Elder went further and said,[2] "Fulfilling the commandment of loving one's fellow Jew is the entire Torah, and the rest (the other commandments) is merely commentary."

The *mitzvah* of *Ahavat Yisrael* and its fulfillment expresses itself not only in practical matters, such as offering help to another, but extends to "matters of the heart," being able to rejoice for someone else's good fortune.

ONE SPIRITUAL BODY

Although it is only one part of the body that derives **enjoyment** from food when eating, in actuality, it is all of the body that derives **benefit** from the food. So, too, with us as a people, we are all one spiritual body—when one person **enjoys** good fortune, we are all **benefitting**, since we are all one entity .

(However, an envious person is one who cannot accept that someone else has something that they desire or has something more than them. He is called a *tzar ayin*, in the language of the Sages, having a narrow, unforgiving, and ungenerous eye. Looking and measuring what others have is the beginning of envy and begins the slippery slope to bitterness and the inability to rejoice in the good fortune of another.

On the other hand, one who is able to accept the good fortune of others (knowing that everything is Divinely ordained) is called a *tov ayin*, a person with a good eye.)

---

1. Leviticus 19:18. See *Rashi* on the verse. See Jerusalem Talmud, *Nedarim* 9:4.

2. *Shabbat* 31a. See *Likkutei Sichot*, vol. 17, p. 219, which explains the difference between the saying of R. Akiva concerning *ahavat Yisrael: Zeh klal gadol batorah*—"This is a great principle of the Torah," and the saying of Hillel concerning *ahavat Yisrael*: *Zu hi kol hatorah, ve'idach pirusha hu*—"This is the entire Torah, the rest being explanation."

A person with *Ahavat Yisrael* is therefore not only able to grieve at their friend's pain, to the point of praying for them (certainly, they would never rejoice in their fellow's failure, G-d forbid), but is able to truly rejoice at his friend's good fortune.

There is a deeper notion of *Ahavat Yisrael* that explains why it is considered such a fundamental part of the Torah, to the extent that Hillel called it the "entire Torah," and this is expounded in Kabbalah and the teachings of Chasidut:[3] The command to love another Jew is not only a commandment involving a specific act; rather, the love itself is the *mitzvah*. On this concept, the question has always been asked: how can love—an emotion—be commanded? Either you love, or you don't. Commanding it won't help create it.

The answer is that the command is to love **every** Jew, and, as the Baal Shem Tov taught, even one we do not know. This type of love is far greater than what we traditionally understand love to be—an emotional connection created with someone with whom we have a relationship. Rather *Ahavat Yisrael* is deeper, based on something that we all share and have in common—something that unites us all.

What we all have in common is our **soul**, the *neshamah*, which is a part of G-d. Every Jew is part of one spiritual "body" since the source of our souls is in the one G-d, and thus, we all have one Father. Therefore, since we all share this kinship of one Father, every one of us is part of one larger spiritual entity. Indeed, it is **only the body that separates** one Jew from his fellow, **but it is the soul that unites us.**

---

3. *Tanya*, ch. 32.

Thus, the focus of this *mitzvah* is on the thing that makes us all **one**, rather than on what separates us.

Since the purpose and the entire aim of the Torah is to value and promote the spiritual over the material—to foster the soul, which should be primary, over the body, which should be secondary—therefore, he who indeed values the soul over the body will love his fellow as he loves himself, for the other **is** himself, the two being **one soul**.

This is why Hillel the Elder said that loving one's fellow Jew is the entire Torah, for that is indeed the entire **purpose** of the Torah: to value and promote the soul over the body. This explains the exemplary *Ahavat Yisrael* that the leaders of our people and the spiritual giants who have been our guides throughout history have all displayed.

Accordingly, when one person and his fellow are unified from this perspective, then a person can certainly rejoice at his fellow's good fortune[4] and be saddened at his failure. (Thus, the commandment to love your fellow as yourself includes loving one who is displeasing and difficult to love by nature.)

Besides the command to love another Jew, there is another great love that we are commanded about in the Torah, which is to "love the L-rd your G-d." This prompted the disciples of the Alter Rebbe to ask him, "Which is the superior divine service—cultivating love of G-d or cultivating love of Israel?" To which he replied, "Both are engraved equally on the soul of every Jew. Nevertheless, since G-d Himself declares,[5] 'I have loved you...,' it follows that love of Israel is superior because it involves

---

4. *Rambam, Hilchot De'ot* 6:3.

5. Malachi 1:2.

loving what one's Beloved loves, and Hashem loves all His children."[6]

Indeed, the Lubavitcher Rebbe would say that, when talking to another Jew, we should remember the saying of the Baal Shem Tov that every Jew is loved by Hashem like an only child born to parents in old age and even more so.

There is an added dimension to the *mitzvah* of *Ahavat Yisrael* that stems from the fact that each one of us brings blessing and salvation to the other. Rambam states that every good deed brings salvation to the entire world.[7] Since "every Jew is full of *mitzvot*, just as a pomegranate is full of seeds," therefore one should feel gratitude and *Ahavat Yisrael* to every Jew, even one whom we have never met, because **each of us receives salvation from the other**.[8]

The importance of the *mitzvah* of loving another Jew carries over to the inverse as well, namely, hating another Jew (G-d forbid). For it is absolutely forbidden to hate any Jew in our heart, and the Torah adds an explicit commandment in this regard, as is stated,[9] "You shall not hate your brother in your heart."

Indeed, it was for the sin of (baseless) hatred more than anything else that the *Beit Hamikdash* was destroyed and we were exiled from our land almost two thousand years ago.[10] (The reason for such dire results is that the greater the importance of the matter (and love of one's fellow Jew is "the entire Torah," as

---

6. *Hayom Yom*, 28 Nissan.

7. *Hilchot Teshuvah* 3:4.

8. *Likkutei Sichot*, vol. 21, p. 51. The question could be asked as follows: something negative done by another can also affect everyone, which would induce the opposite of *Ahavat Yisrael*—see the answer to this in *Likkutei Sichot*, vol. 7, p. 14, fn. 22.

9. Leviticus 19:17.

10. *Yoma* 9b.

mentioned above), the more the *yetzer hara* (evil inclination) fights against it.)

In terms of righting the wrong and "repairing" the lack of *Ahavat Yisrael* that caused the destruction, the resultant exile and dispersion have served to teach us the preciousness of another Jew.

For, after the destruction, we were exiled from our home and scattered to the four corners of the world, lost in strange and inhospitable lands, akin to being lost in a forest. When a person is lost in a forest all alone and encounters someone else in the same predicament, a special bond is created between the two. So, too, is it in our exile and dispersion: each encounter with another Jew, in whatever corner of the world it may be, takes on a far deeper significance, one that expresses itself in the feeling of shared kinship, common identity, and mutual bond of "brotherhood"—the antithesis of what caused the destruction.

Thus the antidote to counteract the syndrome of ("baseless") hatred—*sinat chinam*—is therefore ("baseless") love—*ahavat chinam*.[11]

Therefore, if we were to make a point of thinking only good about each other, then *kemayim hapanim lepanim kein lev ha'adam el ha'adam*[12]—"Just as water reflects back the face reflected in it, so too with the heart of one man to another." **Thinking good of another in one's heart is reflected back from the other heart with reciprocal warm feelings.**

It goes without saying that besides the love which is in the heart, there is also an obligation to help our fellow

11. See *Peleh Yoetz*. See also *Torat Menachem—Hitvaaduyot*, vol. 2, p. 211; *Igrot Kodesh by the Lubavitcher Rebbe*, vol. 4, p. 440.

12. Proverbs 27:19.

in practical matters in any way we can, such as giving to charity, performing good deeds, returning lost objects, helping load or unload a heavy burden when help is needed,[13] and so on. In general, it is a *mitzvah* to help our fellow in any way—carrying his burden together with him (*hanosei b'ol im chavero*).

The *mitzvah* of *Ahavat Yisrael* encompasses not only all manner of physical help but extends also to spiritual matters—to guide another away from wrongdoing and from the wrong path in life as well as bringing another Jewish soul closer to the service of Hashem[14]—since in this matter, all Jews are guarantors of one another.

Our holy Rebbes, especially the Rebbe of our generation, sent emissaries even to places distant from Torah and *mitzvot* in order to bring Jews closer to our heritage and give them the merit of connection to Torah and *mitzvot*.

The Baal Shem Tov taught that a soul may descend to this world and live a whole life, and it could all be just to do a favor, materially or even more so spiritually, for another, so great is the imperative of *Ahavat Yisrael*.[15]

The Rebbe notes that the word *chaim*—life—is plural: literally, it means "lives." We are not truly "alive" until we think and care about others.

13. Exodus 23:5. See *Sefer Hachinuch, Mitzvah 80*: "The Torah's command to "surely help him" requires of us to feel compassionate and merciful to someone suffering, even financial loss, and it is necessary to step in and actively help."

14. Paraphrased from *Sefer Hasichot 5748*, vol. 1, p. 84, ff. This ideal is expressed a multitude of times in numerous sources of Chasidut. See also *Likkutei Sichot*, vol. 6, pp. 274-275.

15. *Igrot Kodesh by R. Yosef Yitzchak*, vol. 3. p. 295. Quoted in *Hayom Yom*, 5 Iyar. See also *Hayom Yom*, 28 Sivan, where the Tzemach Tzedek is quoted as having told his son that all the Heavenly Chambers are opened for the person who helps someone else in his livelihood, even to earn a small amount.

32b

הִמָּנְעוּת מִמְּרִיבוֹת—לְעוֹלָם לֹא לָרִיב, בִּמְיֻחָד לֹא עַל מִצְווֹת

Never quarrel, especially over a *mitzvah*

Our Sages advised us never ever to quarrel, especially over a supposedly “holy” cause. Resist the urge because even if you “win,” you “lose.” Nothing good can come from it.

One should never quarrel[15] and certainly not over supposedly "spiritual" matters, whether communal or personal. (This is where we see that the *yetzer hara* focuses most of its attention, inducing people with the thought that their cause is for holiness.)[16] Similarly, one should never quarrel over *mitzvot*, such as honors in the synagogue, etc. Our Sages tell us that no peace can come from a quarrel.[17]

An example of this can be seen from the eating of the showbread in the *Beit Hamikdash*. Although this was a positive commandment from G-d, only the gluttonous would grab, while the modest would stand to the side.[18]

---

15. It is said that the negative power of disagreement and quarrel—*machloket*—is so great it is likened to fire. It can destroy money, body, and soul. Far better to be from those that hear their shame and do not answer (see *Pele Yoetz: Machloket*).

16. See *Igrot Kodesh by the Alter Rebbe* (Kehot, 2012), pp. 203-204.

17. *Sifri Devarim* 25:1. See *Igrot Kodesh* ibid.

18. *Yoma* 39a. *Shulchan Aruch Harav, Orach Chaim* 53:29.

33

צְדָקָה

Charity

Hashem is "charitable" to us by continuously renewing His creation and granting us life every instant. The ultimate way we can emulate Him is to be charitable one to another.

G-d is charitable to us constantly, each day and at each instant, by continuously renewing His creation and, in this way, giving us our life. One of the ways in which we are able to imitate Him and emulate His ways is by acting charitably and thus giving life, one to another.

The Torah therefore mandates us with a positive commandment to give *tzedakah* to the poor of our People, as the verse states,[1] "You shall open your hand to him, and your brother shall live with you."[2] Being sons of one Father, we are therefore all brothers; if we will not have mercy upon our brother, then who will?

Whoever sees a poor man requesting help and closes his eyes to his plight by not giving him charity has transgressed a negative commandment, as it says,[3] "You shall not harden your heart or close your hand against your destitute brother."

Furthermore, the Baal Shem Tov taught[4] that even if one gives *tzedakah* to a poor man but does not feel his plight, it is like "shedding his blood."

Tzedakah is the highest virtue and is referred to as **the** *mitzvah* (in Hebrew, ***HaMitzvah***, with the emphasis on the first *hey*, known as the "*hey* of distinction") due to its great significance and the fact that it equals all the other *mitzvot*.[5] The Talmud says[6] that *tzedakah* is the strongest force in the world, able to overcome all other forces.

---

1. Deuteronomy 15:8.

2. Leviticus 25:36. See *Rambam, Hilchot Matnot Aniyim* 10:2: "All Jewish people are brothers, as the verse says, 'You are sons to the Lord your G-d, and if you will not show mercy on your brother, then who will?'"

3. Deuteronomy 15:7.

4. *Keter Shem Tov (Hosafot)* §36.

5. *Bava Batra* 9a. See *Kitzur Shulchan Aruch* §34.

6. *Bava Batra* 10a.

One should observe the *mitzvah* of *tzedakah* with great care (even more so than other positive *mitzvot*), for being charitable and giving *tzedakah* is a trait we inherited from Abraham, and it epitomizes one of the main character traits of the Jewish nation.[7]

Perhaps it is for this reason that **when it came to counting the Jewish people, G-d told Moshe not to count them by their numbers, for that is not the real measure of our People. Rather, he was to count them by their contributions.**

The greatness of *tzedakah*, it is explained,[8] stems from the fact that it is in the nature of people to invest all of their energy and spirit into their livelihood. When they then take part of their earnings and dispense *tzedakah* to those in need, they are in effect giving away part of their very life, so to speak, as so much of their time, effort, and toil went into earning that money.

Whereas with other *mitzvot*, their performance typically involves the participation usually of a single limb and limited energy—and then, only during the actual performance of the *mitzvah*—with *tzedakah*, a person is fully engaged from the time he begins working for the money until he gives the *tzedakah*. In this way, he elevates all the energy he expended on earning the money, for it is now devoted to the service of G-d.

Therefore, *tzedakah* is equated with the performance of all the other *mitzvot*.

Furthermore, since the money given to the poor person

7. *Beitzah* 32b. See *Yevamot* 79a: "Three signs..." (*Eiruvin* 65b: "A man is recognized...") and the elucidation according to *drush* quoted in *Kitzur Halachot l'Avot u'Banim*, laws of *Tzedakah*, fn. 4.

8. *Tanya*, chs. 34, 37; *Iggeret Hakodesh*, 3-4. See *Likkutei Sichot*, vol. 1, p. 182.

could have been used by the giver to purchase his own personal necessities, when someone foregoes that and instead contributes it to charity, it is considered as if he offered a sacrifice upon the Altar of the Temple. The reason for this is because there is no greater (personal) sacrifice than this act, which is why *tzedakah* is compared also to all of the sacrificial offerings.[8]

The great gift of the *mitzvah* of *tzedakah* is that it gives us cause to reflect upon a profound truth: any money that we possess is actually not ours; rather, it is a "deposit" from G-d, being held by us for its proper use.

In this way, ***tzedakah* teaches us one of life's ultimate lessons: we may possess things, but we don't own anything. It is all G-d's, and we are just His treasurers.**

This one insight alone is capable of freeing us from the financial insecurities that drive many people. We can be less fearful of losing money knowing that it is not really ours; rather, it belongs to G-d.[9] He is in control of it and dispenses it as He sees fit.

When dispensing to *tzedakah*, one should do so with a kind disposition and *simchah*—joy.[10] For we are acting as G-d's loyal treasurer (in effect, His

JUST A MILLION

It is mistaken to think, as so many do, that the notional "million" in their bank account will make everything right in life. Why fixate on seeking this fictional threshold of happiness? Perhaps it is too much, perhaps it is too little (and why limit G-d?). All one need ask for is that every time one "puts their hand in their pocket," they should find what they need at that moment.

---

9. *Kitzur Shulchan Aruch* 34:1.

10. *Rambam* ibid., 4. *Kitzur Shulchan Aruch* ibid., 7. See *Shulchan Menachem*, vol. 5, p. 106, where it is discussed whether the smile and joyful countenance of the giver when dispensing charity is an essential part of the *mitzvah* or an added embellishment. R. Schneur Zalman of Liadi was concerned for the feelings of those in need of charity and insisted that it not be called "charity," rather a "loan" or "*gemillut chesed*" (See *Igrot Kodesh by R. Yosef Yitzchak*, vol. 8, p. 605).

hand), doing with the money exactly what G-d wanted to be done with it.

An underlying principle regarding *tzedakah* is that **a person does not become poor from giving charity,**[11] **for G-d will repay the giver even double what he gave** (as the verse says,[12] "There is one who scatters, and he gathers more"). Nor will harm or damage come as a result of giving to *tzedakah* (as it says,[13] "*Tzedakah* fosters peace").

Furthermore, the Alter Rebbe taught[14] that **the act of *tzedakah* refines the mind and the heart of the giver a "thousandfold."**

Similarly, the Talmud tells us[15] that the famous R. Elazar would seek out the poor before prayers each day in order to give to *tzedakah* and only then would he begin to pray. The Talmud is teaching us that **by giving "life" in this world to a poor man before praying, then measure for measure, a person's prayers become infused with "life" from the upper worlds above and break through all barriers.**

Therefore, one should not hesitate to give to *tzedakah*.

Even one who is poor himself is obligated to give to *tzedakah*.[16] **The Torah understood that giving is a basic human need, lending dignity to life, and even a poor man feels his dignity restored by giving in some way.**

If a person does not have any funds to give, he should

---

11. *Rambam* ibid., 2. It is explained that when we give money to the poor we are actually "lending" the money to G-d, Who will certainly repay His "loan."

12. Proverbs 11:24.

13. Isaiah 32:17.

14. *Torah Or, Bereishit* 1b.

15. *Bava Batra* 10a. See *Hayom Yom*, 2 Kislev.

16. *Kitzur Shulchan Aruch* ibid., 2.

at least speak to the needy individual in a caring and sensitive manner and at all times be careful not to embarrass him.

The Talmud relates[17] that King Munbaz (who according to one opinion was a convert to Judaism) opened his storehouses and distributed his wealth to the poor during a period of famine. His family came to him and protested, saying, "Your fathers accumulated wealth and continuously expanded their storehouses. However, not only do you not save anything, but you are squandering everything!"

Munbaz responded, "My actions are more praiseworthy than theirs. For they stockpiled in this world, but I, through my charitable acts, am stockpiling in Heaven (where the main reward for his charity was accumulating, in addition to the blessings he would merit to receive in this world).

"Furthermore, my ancestors stored their wealth in places where others could steal it, but I am storing in a place that no one can reach (his actions were recorded and stored under G-d's throne). My ancestors stored wealth that didn't produce anything, but I've stored up wealth that produces fruits. (For *tzedakah* is counted among the items that one reaps the benefits and profits not only in this world, but the principle remains for the World to Come).

"My ancestors stockpiled money, while I've stockpiled lives (for one who saves the life of a poor person with *tzedakah* is credited with giving him life).

"My ancestors stockpiled wealth from which they had

17. *Bava Batra* 11a.

no enjoyment in their life (they were saving for those who would follow them), but I have accumulated the reward of my *tzedakah* for myself.

"My ancestors stored gold and silver to enjoy in this world, but I stored merits for the World to Come."

Regarding *tzedakah*, our Sages taught:[18] "When someone has compassion for others, Heaven has compassion for him." The Talmud relates[19] that R. Akiva was informed by astrologers that his daughter was destined to pass away on her wedding day. R. Akiva was gravely concerned about this prediction until he visited her the morning after her wedding and found her alive. Upon investigating, it was discovered that when she had removed her hair pin before going to bed and stuck it into the wall, she had unknowingly pierced a snake and killed it.

Her father asked her, "What good deed did you perform that saved you from certain death?" She responded, "Last evening while everyone was preoccupied with the wedding festivities, they failed to notice a pauper in need of food. I spotted him and gave him my own portion from the wedding meal." R. Akiva exclaimed, "Ah! You performed the *mitzvah* of *tzedakah*!" He then went out and taught: "(the *mitzvah* of) *tzedakah* saves from death and contributes life."

Just as a person spends money daily for his own personal needs, so should a person also expend funds on behalf of G-d's needs, i.e., the poor. And since everyone needs

---

18. *Shabbat* 151b. See *Hayom Yom*, 28 Sivan, citing the *Tzemach Tzedek*, that all the Heavenly Chambers are opened for the person who helps someone else in his livelihood, even to earn a small amount (cited also above, section 32a, fn. 15).

19. *Shabbat* 156b.

mercy from Above at all times, therefore, by thinking of those less fortunate and displaying compassion for them here in this world below, we elicit compassion upon ourselves from Above.

A person should accustom himself to give *tzedakah* daily.[20]

(The Lubavitcher Rebbe suggested that a *tzedakah* box be affixed to the wall of our home (in a visible place, such as the kitchen, so that we are reminded of the need to be charitable), and in this way, the *tzedakah* box becomes an actual part of the home, thereby transforming the entire house to a "home of *tzedakah*.")[21]

There are eight levels in the mitzvah of giving *tzedakah*:[22]

1) The highest level of *tzedakah* is when one assists a poor man by giving him a gift or a loan that puts him on his feet. Similar to this is if one partners with him in a business venture in order to help him or finds employment for the poor man so that he can become self-sufficient.

2) A lower level is when neither the giver nor the recipient is aware of each other's identity. Thus, the donor has no expectations about obtaining a return favor from the recipient, and the latter is saved from any embarrassment since he doesn't know the donor.

3) One degree lower is when only the benefactor knows the identity of the recipient, like the great

---

20. *Birkei Yosef* 10:247. See *Shulchan Menachem*, vol. 5, p. 102.

21. *Torat Menachem—Hitvaaduyot 5748*, vol. 4, p. 345. See *Shulchan Menachem*, vol. 5, p. 118.

22. *Rambam* ibid., 7. *Kitzur Shulchan Aruch* 34:7,12,13.

Sages who would leave money anonymously at the doorsteps of the poor.

4) A lower level is when the recipient alone is aware of the identity of the benefactor. Such was the case with some of the great Sages who would scatter bundles of money behind them as they walked among the poor, thus ensuring that they were not aware of who received their *tzedakah*.

5) One level lower is when one gives before he is asked.

6) Lower still is the level when one gives after he is asked.

7) Even lower is the level where one gives less than an appropriate amount but with a good disposition.

8) The lowest level is when one gives to *tzedakah*, but begrudgingly.

So how much charity should one give? The accepted amount that meets the measure of charity is at least one-tenth (10%) of one's earnings. Those who seek to give one-fifth (20%) are exemplary.[23] More than one-fifth, says the Talmud,[24] one should not expend on charity.

It is explained, however,[25] that this ruling applies only to one who has no need to rectify and atone for misdeeds of the past. **But should a person still need to remedy his soul and rectify such matters of the past, then he should give more than this measure, even without measure.**

23. See *Shulchan Menachem*, vol. 5, p. 83 (also pp. 89-124).

24. *Ketubot* 50a.

25. *Iggeret Hakodesh*, 10.

This prescribed remedy works, and the "sacrifice" involved in giving charity cleanses the soul of blemishes caused both in the upper as well as lower worlds because the light of charity has a unique power, radiating and extending infinitely throughout all the worlds.

When it comes to healing a person's body, we see that a person will spend any amount ("All that a man has, he will give on behalf of his life").[26] If so, then surely healing of the soul is not inferior, and a person should give even more than a fifth of his earnings to charity.

R. Schneur Zalman of Liadi taught[27] that the main "*avodat Hashem*"—service of G-d—in our times is "*avodat hatzedakah*"—serving Hashem with the mitzvah of *tzedakah*, as our Sages teach us:[28] "Israel will only be redeemed through charity."

In addition to helping another monetarily, we can also perform charity by giving of our time and energy, assisting another or doing them a favor.

Furthermore, assisting someone in spiritual matters by bringing them closer to Torah and *mitzvot* is a very great form of *tzedakah*.[29]

26. *Iyov* 2:4. See *Iggeret Hateshuvah*, end ch. 3.

27. *Iggeret Hakodesh*, 9.

28. *Shabbat* 139a.

29. *Torat Menachem—Hitvaaduyot*, vol. 1, p. 211.

34

הַכְנָסַת אוֹרְחִים

The *mitzvah* of hospitality

We are all "guests" in Hashem's world. He personally provides us with all our needs during our "stay." By hosting guests and satisfying their needs, we are thus able to emulate Hashem and His ways.

Receiving and welcoming guests is part of the broader *mitzvah* of *chesed*, which is itself included in the broader commandment to *walk in the ways of Hashem*, i.e., to imitate Hashem's ways.

Since we are all guests in Hashem's world[1] and Hashem personally provides us with all our needs, our act of hosting guests in our home and satisfying their needs is one of the highest forms of imitating Hashem's ways.

This *mitzvah* was promulgated by Abraham our father, who, in his kindness, would feed and give water to passersby and accompany them on the road.[2]

Receiving and hosting guests is considered even greater than receiving the presence of Hashem Himself.

This is learned from the story of G-d's visit to Abraham after the circumcision, when suddenly, three guests appeared, and Abraham put aside his conversation with Hashem to run and greet the guests[3] (as is stated:[4] "And [Abraham] said, 'Hashem, if I have found favor in Your eyes, please do not pass from before your servant'").

It is interesting to note that the service that Abraham himself performed for the guests (personally serving them bread) was reciprocated later directly by Hashem to his children in the desert (in the form of the manna, which descended directly from Heaven each day to each family). However, that which was served to Abraham's guests indirectly, through a servant (such

1. As elucidated according to *Maharal*.

2. *Rambam, Hilchot Avel* 14:1.

3. *Shabbat* 117a. *Shavuot* 35b. Also *Rashi* on Genesis 18:3. *Rambam* ibid., 2.

4. Genesis ibid.

as the water, which was fetched by a helper), was later also given to the Jews in the desert in an indirect way.

Furthermore, receiving guests is included in those things that one is rewarded for even in this world and whose everlasting reward is received in the World to Come.[5]

Our Sages say:[6] "In the times of the *Beit Hamikdash*, the Altar would atone for man. Now that there is no *Beit Hamikdash*, a person's own table atones for him when he receives and feeds guests at his table."

This *mitzvah* is fulfilled with guests from another city specifically (and from one's own city if the guest is solitary, has no household, and so forth). However, guests from one's own city in the form of a gathering of friends is not considered an obligatory *mitzvah* feast for guests but rather a voluntary meal.[7]

The main thing in fulfilling this *mitzvah* is that the guests should be greeted with pleasantness and a smile. **The focus of our hospitality ought to be (not so much on the objects that one does the *mitzvah* with, such as the food and drink the guests will eat, but rather) on the person, the guest himself, who should be made to feel welcome.**[8]

We should also escort guests a little way (four *amot*[9]—a little more than six feet) from the front door when bidding them farewell. This is the *mitzvah* of *leviyah*—accompanying guests.

5. *Peah* 1:1. *Shabbat* ibid.

6. *Menachot* 97a. (See the *Shitah Mekubetzet* there, fn. 2).

7. *Shulchan Aruch Harav, Orach Chaim* 307:23; 333:6; 510:20.

8. *Likkutei Sichot*, vol. 25, p. 78. See *Kitzur Halachot L'Avot u'Banim, Hilchot Shabbat*, 20:9: *Hachnasat Orchim*.

9. See *Oholecha Ba'amitcha* 7:26.

This gesture is considered a protective spiritual aid for the guest in order that no harm befall them on their way. This was especially so in times when people would travel alone in unpopulated areas.

Furthermore, in this way, the host completes the *mitzvah* of *hachnasat orchim*, which is comprised of the three elements *achilah*, *shetiyah*, and *leviyah*—eating, drinking, and accompanying. These are hinted at in the word *aishel* ("...and Abraham planted an *aishel*"), which is comprised of the letters *aleph*, *shin*, and *lamed* and stands for these three elements: the *aleph* referring to *achilah*, the *shin* to *shetiyah*, and the *lamed* to *leviyah*.

Also, when a guest leaves his host, it is possible that the guest may feel that the host tired of him and wished him to leave, so by accompanying him, the host shows that he would really like to have spent more time with the guest, and in this way, the guest will leave with positive feelings.

35a

בִּקּוּר חוֹלִים

Visiting the sick

Whatever Hashem asks of us, He does Himself. When Hashem teaches us to visit the sick, He does so Himself, for the *Shechinah*, the Divine Presence, comes and stands above the bed of the sick. Visiting someone who is sick is therefore not only emulating Hashem and joining Him in the visit but also helping to revive the spirit of the patient, who senses the care and concern expressed in this gesture.

The *mitzvah* of visiting the sick is part of the general *mitzvah* of performing *chesed*—acts of kindness. *Rambam* states that it is part of the *mitzvah* of *Ahavat Yisrael*.

The kindness involved in visiting the sick is so great that the Talmud[1] tells us it is one of the six *mitzvot* whose "fruits" we get to partake of in this world, and its "principal" is retained for us in the World to Come.

This act of kindness is one of the ways in which we are able to emulate Hashem, for the Talmud[2] says that the *Shechinah*, the Divine Presence, comes and stands above the bed of the sick. The Torah records[3] that Hashem Himself visited Abraham our father on the third day following his circumcision.

The mitzvah of visiting the sick involves three components: our **body**, our **soul**, and our **money**:

It is performed with our **body** not only by paying a personal visit but actually doing things that uplift the spirit, and give comfort to, the patient.

The Talmud tells us[4] that when R. Akiva noticed that one of his students had been absent for a few days from the study hall, he went personally to inquire about him. When he came to the house of the student, he found him sick and unkempt, and the house in disarray. R.

1. *Shabbat* 127a.

2. *Nedarim* 40a.

3. Genesis 18:1. The Torah alludes to the centrality of kindness in life and its place in our understanding of G-d's ways in the fact that the Torah commences and closes with narratives describing acts of kindness performed by G-d Himself. The beginning of the Torah relates that Hashem made garments for Adam and Eve, and the end relates that He buried Moshe. In this connection, it has been pointed out that the *gematria* (numerical value) of the word ***Torah*** in Hebrew is equivalent to the numerical value of the Hebrew word ***gemilut chasadim***—acts of kindness.

4. *Nedarim* ibid.

Akiva, despite the fact that he was the leader of the generation and could have arranged for others to assist the patient, nevertheless, he himself proceeded to bathe the student, change his bedding, and clean the room. The student proclaimed to R. Akiva, "Rebbi, *hechyisani*—you have brought me back to life!", and as a result of which, R. Akiva went on to teach that he who does not visit the sick is akin to shedding blood.

The *mitzvah* is also performed with our **soul** by praying for the sick and wishing and blessing them with a speedy recovery (*refuah shelaimah*) before leaving them.

And it is performed with our **money** by helping with medical expenses if necessary, which would bring the sick peace of mind and also, it has been suggested, by giving charity on their behalf.

35b

נִחוּם אֲבֵלִים

Comforting those in mourning

Comforting the mourner is a kindness for the living and for the dead. By stressing the supremacy and the eternal nature of the soul in our words of solace, we bring comfort to the mourner. This also brings comfort to the soul of the departed, which ascends to be with G-d. It worries for the body, its faithful companion for so long, which it has left behind and now descends to dust. Recalling the spiritual achievements of the departed in our words of comfort helps vindicate their life in this world, thus comforting the soul for its now departed companion.

The *mitzvah* of comforting the mourner is also one of the ways in which we are able to emulate Hashem and go in his ways. As the Torah tells us,[5] G-d Himself went to comfort Isaac after the passing of his father, Abraham. It is part of the general *mitzvah* of performing *chesed*—acts of kindness. Rambam states that it is part of the *mitzvah* of *Ahavat Yisrael*.

The mitzvah of comforting a mourner also brings comfort to the soul of the departed,[6] which is in mourning for the body that was its faithful servant throughout its sojourn in this world and with which it fulfilled *mitzvot*. While the meritorious soul ascends to Heaven to reconnect to G-d, the body goes to a place of dust.

Thus, the *mitzvah* of comforting the mourner is unique in that it is a kindness to both the living as well as the dead.

Furthermore, this *mitzvah* represents the epitome of the command to follow the ways of Hashem and to emulate Him.[7]

For those giving comfort to the mourner speak about the eternal nature of the soul, how after death, it lives on, no longer limited by the constraints of the body. The connection between the departed and the family in mourning thus continues from the point of view of the soul, which is the essence of the person. (Moreover, in the future, the great resurrection of all those who have passed will take place, reuniting us with the past generations—one of our cardinal beliefs.)

---

5. Genesis 25:11. See *Rashi* on *Sotah* 14a.

6. See end *Shabbat* 152a and *Maharsha* there.

7. See *Torat Menachem—Menachem Tzion*, vol. 1, p. 3.

All these concepts stress one thing: how the "spirit" is primary and the "material" is secondary. In this way, the mitzvah of comforting the mourner actually expresses the entire ethos of Torah values and thereby epitomizes the command to emulate G-d and to go in His ways.

(So, too, assisting with the burial of the dead is one of the ways in which we are able to emulate Hashem and go in his ways. For we see that G-d Himself buried the dead, as we find He did for Moshe, as mentioned in the footnotes to section 35a.

This example has been continued throughout the generations in the institution of the *Chevra Kadisha*—Holy Society, in all Jewish communities, who prepare a deceased Jew for the awesome moment when, having taken leave of his body, he returns to his Maker.

Caring for another Jew, even after his departure from this world, is the greatest act of *chesed*, being a kindness that cannot be repaid, and is therefore termed *chesed shel emet*—true kindness. It reflects our deep belief in the eternality of the Jewish soul as well as the eternality of the Jewish body, which will come to fulfillment when "death will disappear..." and the great resurrection will take place.)

36

לֹא תַעֲמֹד עַל דַּם רֵעֶךָ—
לֹא לַעֲמוֹד בְּחֹסֶר מַעַשׂ כַּאֲשֶׁר
דָּמוֹ שֶׁל מִישֶׁהוּ נִשְׁפָּךְ

Not standing idly by while the blood of one's fellow is being spilled

---

The Torah forbids us to stand by when someone is in danger, whether physically or spiritually, without attempting to rescue them. We are all responsible one for another. We cannot choose "not to get involved." It is an absolute obligation to try to rescue our brother who is "drowning." If not, we shed his blood and in this way destroy the world, for life has infinite value, and each person is equal to the entire world.

Someone who sees a Jew in danger, such as drowning, G-d forbid, must try to rescue him (as is stated:[1] *Lo ta'amod al dam rei'acha*—"Do not stand by (while) the blood of your fellow [is spilled]").

The rationale behind this *mitzvah* is explained in the Talmud,[2] where the Sages made the following observation explaining why G-d created the animal kingdom in pairs, yet mankind, Adam, was created alone: "Man was created alone to teach that anyone who destroys one life is considered by the Torah as if he has destroyed the entire world, for all of mankind descends from Adam, and anyone who preserves one life is considered by the Torah as if he has preserved the entire world."

Thus, on account of the **infinite value of a human life**, we are prohibited from standing by when someone's life is in danger, and we are obligated to make every effort to rescue them.

It is explained[3] that this refers not only to rescuing someone physically but also (and all the more so) to rescuing a Jew from spiritual harm and "drowning," so to speak, if he is bereft of Torah and *mitzvot*. We are obligated to rescue such a soul by drawing him close to Torah and *mitzvot*. **Ultimately, we are responsible one for another.**

HELP!

The obligation to help another Jew in spiritual need is as great as the obligation to help someone in physical need. It is thus a "life and death" obligation no less than the duty to help a drowning person. Just as with a drowning person, we cannot choose "not to get involved," but we are obliged to help, so, too, in spiritual matters, it is our obligation to reach out and help "rescue" another. With the Jewish people, if you lose the **spiritual**, you end up losing the **physical**—it is all one.

1. Leviticus 19:16.
2. *Sanhedrin* 37a.
3. *Likkutei Sichot*, vol. 32, p. 125. See sources and comments quoted in fn. 35 there. See *Minchat Chinuch* quoted in the aforementioned sources, on *Mitzvah* 239.

37

לָדוּן אֶת כָּל הָאָדָם לְכַף זְכוּת

Judging everyone favorably

Hashem believes in us—He sees the good in us. Our job is to see the good in others—to see them as G-d sees them, judging them favorably and giving them the benefit of any doubt.

It is a positive *mitzvah* to judge everyone favorably[1] (as is stated:[2] "In righteousness, judge your people").

Even though the commandment is mainly for court judges, it also includes any situation in which a person sees someone doing something that could be interpreted either positively or negatively, in which case one is obligated to judge it positively, to the favorable side.[3] Indeed, the Mishnah says,[4] "Judge every man favorably." There are those who say that this is a prerequisite and a "gate" to all the other *mitzvot* between man and his fellow.[5]

The Baal Shem Tov taught[6] that when judging another person, one is judging oneself, be it positively or negatively.

BEFORE YOU JUDGE...

The saying: *Hevei don et kol ha'adam l'kaf zechut*, literally translated as: "Judge all people favorably," can also be read with emphasis on the word "*kol*"—*Hevay don et* ***kol*** *ha'adam l'kaf zechut*—"Judge **all** of the other person favorably." This implys that before judging someone else, one needs to take into account **all** of that person, not just what he did—the act in isolation...but the person's whole state of affairs and situation in life, what his background is, education, etc., so that one can indeed judge fairly and with kindness.

---

1. *Sefer Mitzvot Gadol* and *Sefer Mitvot Katan. Rambam, Sefer Hamitzvot, Mitzvah 177.*

2. Leviticus 19:16.

3. See *Rambam, Sefer Hamitzvot*, ibid. *Shavuot* 30a: The command in the Torah is: *B'tzedek tishpot amitecha*—"With righteousness you shall judge your friend"—judge your friend favorably—*l'kaf zechut*. See *Rashi* there, caption: *L'kaf zechut*: The Torah is not referring to judges in a court (*baalai din*), rather to the relationship between man and man. When one sees someone doing something that could be judged either positively or negatively, we are commanded not to judge that person negatively and assume he is sinning. Rather, we are commanded to judge him positively.

Furthermore, it is explained that when one does think good of another, three *mitzvot* are being fulfilled: 1) *Betzedek tishpot amitecha*—"Judge another favorably," 2) *Lo tisna et achicha bilvovecha*—"Do not hate your brother in your heart," and 3) *V'ahavta l'reiacha kamocha*—"You shall love your neighbor like yourself." For this reason, therefore, reward is received for each instant that one thinks favorably of another, while the opposite is true of one who chooses to think negatively of another.

4. *Avot* 1:6. See *Tanya*, ch. 30, where it is explained that one should bear in mind before judging someone else that "his place and his occupation caused him to be the way he is."

5. *Shaloh*, who notes that this *mitzvah* of *Betzdek tishpot amitecha*, is the first *mitzvah* of all the *mitzvot* "between man and his fellow" that are listed in *Parashat Kedoshim*.

6. *Keter Shem Tov (Hosafot)* §149.

Being judgmental about another, even if it is justifying another's suffering because of perceived misdeeds or character flaws in the other person, actually brings "judgment" upon oneself. The proper reaction is to feel the other person's pain, have compassion, and pray for them in order to awaken mercy for the one suffering. One who "joins" in the pain of his friend in this way is similarly rewarded from Heaven with compassion.

It is explained[7] that the power of "judgment" is so great that the favorable judgment of another actually affects the other person in a positive way, revealing the good hidden within him and his latent potential to do good.

(This is especially so when the good is verbalized because speech has the power to reveal that which is hidden, as it reveals and expresses whatever is hidden within the heart and mind.)

The importance of seeing and bringing out the latent good in another can be learned from Hashem Himself, Who did this when He created the world.

In the account of creation as set out in *Bereishit*, the Torah says that after each thing was created, G-d

"WHO IS WISE...?"

The Ba'al Shem Tov taught us to remember the words of the *Mishnah* that says *Elzehu chacham? Halomed mikol adam*—"Who is wise? He who learns from everyone," implying that the wise man knows he is not perfect, and when he sees something apparently negative in his friend, rather than judge him, he understands that this is a lesson from Heaven that he should remedy and repair this issue within **himself**, and in this way, he "learns from everyone." (See section 39 further on for a fuller explanation of this topic.)

---

7. *Likkutei Sichot*, vol. 27, p. 165. (See also *Biurim L'Pirkei Avot*, vol. 1, p. 56). In this talk, the Rebbe emphasizes that when our Sages said *Hevay dan et kol ha'adam l'chaf zechut*—judge everyone favorably is not just a nice frame of mind for the one judging, rather it actually helps the one being judged. A person's favorable judgment of another should be to the extent that it becomes a *zechut*—an actual merit—for the person he is judging and in this way actually adds to the store of the judged person's positive abilities, thus bringing out the good in him.

stepped back, so to speak, and looked at His creation, and "**G-d saw that it was good.**" **He paid it a compliment**, as if to say: "You know...you're good." But surely, everything G-d does is good! Would He make something bad? And why would the verse say: "And He 'saw' that it was good." Just say: "And it was good."

The answer, it has been suggested, is specifically in order to teach us that we too should **"see" the good in others**. In this way, we are truly "walking in His ways" and emulating Him in His traits.

Furthermore, by seeing the good in others, we help the other person see themselves in the "mirror" of our positive opinion, and they can then can grow to become that vision. This can help bring out another dimension of creativity in their soul by opening them to their potential. This too is part of the work of creation, by making someone else "creative."

We are furthermore taught that he who judges his fellow favorably is judged favorably in Heaven.[8]

An example of favorable judgment appears in the Talmud:[9] A hired worker (some say it was R. Akiva before he began studying Torah[10]) was hired by a certain employer (some say it was R. Eliezer ben Horkanus) for three years of work.

At the end of the three years, on Erev Yom Kippur, the worker said, "Give me my pay, and I will go and feed my family." The employer said, "I have no money." The worker replied, "Then give me fruit." The employer

8. *Shabbat* 127b.

9. See ibid., and the two associated stories there. See also *Taanit* 21b; *Likkutei Sichot*, vol. 27, p. 158. See also *Kaf Zechut* and other works.

10. *Teshuvot Rameh MiPano* §63, in the name of the *She'iltot* (quoted in *Ein Yaakov Hamevuar*, vol. 2, p. 539).

said, "I don't have fruit." The worker said, "Then give me land." The employer said, "I have none." The worker said, "Then give me an animal." The employer said, "I don't have any." "Then give me pillows and quilts." "I have none."

When the worker saw he could expect nothing from the employer, he went home with sorrow, embarrassed to face his family emptyhanded after three years.

After Sukkot, the employer took money in his hand and three donkeys, one laden with food, one with drink, and one with delicacies, and went to the home of the worker to pay him his due.

After he was paid and they ate and drank, the employer said: "When you told me that you needed pay and I said I had no money, what did you think?" The worker said, "I thought perhaps you gained access to cheap commodities and purchased them suddenly with the money you had on hand." "And when I said I had no animal?" "I thought perhaps the animal I saw on your land was rented to others." "And when I said I had no land?" "I thought perhaps your land was rented to others." "And when I said I had no fruit?" "I thought perhaps you had not yet taken *maaser* (tithe) from your fruit." "And when I said I had no pillows and quilts?" "I thought perhaps you had consecrated all of your belongings to Hashem, rendering them forbidden for use."

The employer said, "Indeed! That is what happened. I had made a vow to give all of my possessions to the *Beit Hamikdash* because of my son Horkanus, who was not studying Torah (I hoped that in the merit of my gift he would mend his ways). Therefore, I had nothing with which to pay you until I went to the Sages and they pardoned my vows (and that is why I can pay you now). And as for you," said the employer, "just as you judged me favorably, so will Hashem judge you favorably."

38

אִסּוּר רְכִילוּת, לָשׁוֹן הָרָע, וּמוֹצִיא שֵׁם רָע

The prohibition against tale-bearing, gossip, and slander

The Torah forbids gossip, malicious talk, and slander because speech has great power. G-d created the world with speech. If it is positive, it can create worlds and build people, bringing out their hidden good. If it is negative, it can destroy, and, like the proverbial arrow, once spoken, it cannot be brought back. A good rule of thumb with speech is to think beforehand: Is it true, is it kind, and is it necessary?

Speech is very powerful. There is positive speech and there is negative speech. Speech can build, or it can destroy. Therefore, great care must be taken when speaking. The Torah and our Sages actually categorized negative speech into different types.

1) *Rechilut*. It is forbidden to gossip, as is stated in the Torah:[1] "A talebearer shall not go among your people," that is, to go from person to person saying, "This is what so-and-so said about you." This is called *rechilut*. Even if it is true and the words do not cast a negative light, nevertheless, because it is something personal, the talebearer can cause hate between people, and this destroys the world.[2]

2) *Lashon Hara*. There is a worse transgression than talebearing, and that is *lashon hara* (literally, "the evil tongue"), which is to speak negatively of someone, even though you may be saying the truth.

This is such a great sin that the Sages said, "Idol worship, licentiousness, and murder—*lashon hara* is equal to all three."[3]

Lashon hara is like the proverbial arrow which, once shot, can never be brought back. In fact, the Talmud tells us[4] that "the arrow of *lashon hara* 'released' (i.e.: spoken) in Rome kills in Suria."

---

1. Leviticus 19:16.

2. As occurred in the story of Doeg and Achimelech (I Samuel, chs. 21 and 22; see also Psalms 52). Doeg would sing the praises of King David in front of King Saul, ascribing to David qualities that Saul lacked, only in order to provoke Saul's jealousy. Doeg informed Saul that David, who had fled from Saul's jealous anger, had been sheltered by Achimelech and the priests of the city of Nob. Saul had them all killed. This led in the end also to the death not only of Doeg (and Achimelech) but of Saul as well. From this story can be seen how *rechilut*—gossip and talebearing—can destroy the world since each Jew is "an entire world."

3. See *Erchin* 15b. See also *Rambam, Hilchot De'ot* 7:3.

4. *Bereishit Rabbah* 98:3. Jerusalem Talmud, *Peah* 1:1.

So injurious is *lashon hara* and the repercussions of this issue are so intense that it has shaped the destiny of our people as we find when the Torah describes how our fathers perished in the desert, rather than be allowed to enter the Land of Israel. It was only because of *lashon hara*: the spies had said negative things about the land, and the people listened to it.

We further find in the Talmud:[5] "The generation of David was all righteous, but because they were informers and spoke *lashon hara*, when they went out to war, many fell in battle. (Thus, *lashon hara* is so powerful that it can erase the merits of a lifetime of Torah learning and *mitzvah* observance, G-d forbid.) The generation of Achav, on the other hand, were idol worshippers, but since they were not informers and spoke no *lashon hara*, they went out to war and were victorious without casualties."

Our Sages say,[6] "*Lashon hara* kills three—the one who says it, the one who hears it, and the one it is spoken about."

The question is asked: Since the person about whom the *lashon hara* is spoken—the subject of the *lashon hara*—neither spoke it nor heard it and is an innocent "bystander," why should he suffer?

It is explained[7] that this is because **the nature of speech is to reveal what was previously concealed in thought.**

So, if there was some negative trait hidden within the person who is the subject of the *lashon hara*, and this

5. Jerusalem Talmud, ibid.

6. *Erchin* 15b. The Sages say that the one who accepts *lashon hara* is worse than the one who says it.

7. *Likkutei Sichot*, vol. 5, p. 45; vol. 15, p. 32; vol. 27, p. 165.

is now revealed in this world, two things happen to that person:

First, there is a change in Heaven, where the person who is the subject of the *lashon hara* is now viewed differently than before the *lashon hara* revealed his hidden negativity.

Even though Hashem in His compassion sees the good in each person as their true essence, nevertheless, the negative trait that was previously hidden is now revealed in this world. Since the upper and lower worlds move in tandem, this "negativity" has to be taken into account in Heaven, where it is now brought before the Heavenly court and scrutinized.

If it would have remained hidden, then Hashem would have left the matter in abeyance waiting for the person to do *teshuvah* and repent for his negativity.

Second, there is a change within the person himself who is the subject of the *lashon hara*. Verbalizing someone else's negativity brings it out into the open and thus actualizes it, and it will manifest itself in the behavior of the person who is the subject of the *lashon hara*—he will begin to behave that way.

So, even the person who is the subject of *lashon hara* is affected negatively (in these two ways).

The story is told in the Talmud[8] that R. Alexandri would call out, "Who wants life? Who wants life?" Many would gather around him saying, "Give us life!" and he responded, "Who desires life? Protect your tongue from evil."[9]

8. *Avodah Zarah* 19b.

9. Psalms 34:13-14.

(There are cases when a person is permitted and indeed supposed to speak out, even though the information may be disparaging. Specifically, if a person's intent in sharing the negative information is for a positive, constructive, and beneficial purpose (*l'to'elet*), then the prohibition against *lashon hara* does not apply.

For example, if the *lashon hara* serves as a warning to prevent the possibility of future harm or to exonerate the subject of any wrongdoing that he or she may originally have been accused of, then it is considered *l'to'elet*. It is important to note that even with positive intentions, there are many important limitations regarding when it is permitted to speak *lashon hara*, and it is therefore necessary to be knowledgeable in these laws.)

3) *Motzei Shem Ra*. Besides *rechilut* (gossip) and *lashon hara* (talking negatively about someone, even if true), there is a third sin involving speech, and this is the worst of all—*motzei shem ra*—slander, which is to tell malicious lies about another. This has the effect of "murdering" the good name of another. Under no circumstances is this ever permitted.

4) *Onaat Devarim*. A fourth category of negative speech is known as *onaat devarim*, words that cause emotional pain, anger, or embarrassment. This is forbidden, as the Torah says, "Do not aggrieve your fellow man" (this is explained in section 46).

These first four categories are all prohibited by the Torah.

5) *Avak Lashon Hara*. A fifth category of negative speech was included by the Sages in the transgression

of prohibited speech and is known as *avak lashon hara*—literally "the dust of *lashon hara*," a term chosen by the Sages to indicate speech that borders on *lashon hara*, the way dust is like soil, but is not soil itself. This would be saying something whose implied meaning is derogatory or harmful, i.e., speaking gossip through hints and not in a clear way.

Examples of *avak lashon hara*: If one says, "Isn't it amazing so-and-so has become what he is today?"—this could be interpreted either as praise or criticism. Or if one would say, "Don't speak about so-and-so, I don't wish to reveal what I know." Even to praise one's fellow before those who hate him is also in this category because it causes them to speak negatively about him.[10]

6) *Lashon Tov*. However, to speak a person's praise before those who love him is permitted, and we find that **our Sages spoke the praises of their colleagues and students, in this way revealing the hidden good latent within their colleagues and students. For verbalizing someone else's goodness actualizes it by bringing it out into the open.**

In general, a good rule to follow before speaking is to consider for an instant whether what one is about to say is **true**, **necessary**, and **kind** (i.e., free of talebearing, gossip, and slander and will not cause pain to another).

The Baal Shem Tov taught[11] that hearing something negative about another Jew should cause one distress, for either way the situation is painful. If what was said

---

10. See *Rambam* (*Pirush La'am*) *Hilchot De'ot* 7:4 (fns. 7, 8, and 9). See *Bava Batra* 165a: "Most (fall prey) to theft, a few to immorality, but all are trapped in *avak* (the dust of) *lashon hara*."

11. *Keter Shem Tov (Hosafot)* §149.

about the other person is **true**, then that person is not in a good situation. If what was said about the other person is **not true**, then the speaker—the one telling the negative report—is not in a good situation.

39

עַיִן טוֹב—שֶׁלֹּא לִרְאוֹת אֶת הָרָע וְהַשְּׁלִילִי בַּזּוּלָת

Not seeing the negative in another

Thought can be even more powerful than speech, for it affects one's surroundings. In fact, it affects the entire world. Nothing is hidden from Hashem. Everything is open and revealed before Him, even the thoughts of the mind. We need to think good of others, look for the good in them and in every situation, and this will bring out the good within them. It is worth remembering that "thoughts become things."

Just as there is *lashon hara* in **speech**, so, in a certain sense, is there "*lashon hara*" in **thought**—thinking negatively of another.[1]

The Baal Shem Tov taught[2] that when we see bad in another, this is proof that (something like) that bad is to be found in ourselves as well.[3]

Just like looking into a mirror—if your face is clean, you see a clean face (and thus a completely righteous man, who has no evil within, sees no evil in any man[4]), but if your face is unclean, then one sees blemishes in the mirror as well. Really, the faults you see in another are your own faults.

It is explained[5] that since everything that takes place is by divine providence and not by accident (G-d forbid), a person cannot say that he was brought to see the negativity within another by accident.

Rather, there must be some lesson in it.[6]

The reason someone has been shown the negativity of his friend is in order that he can correct it, both in his friend and (mainly) within himself.

The reason he is shown this flaw in his friend and not in himself is alluded to in the words of our Sages:[7] "One's self-love can cover up any transgression" and[8] "One sees all flaws except one's own," for there

---

1. See *Iggeret Hakodesh*, 22, end: "Thinking *lashon hara* of another is worse than saying it."

2. *Me'or Einayim* beginning *Parashat Chukat*. Other sources. See also *Sefer Hasichot Kayitz 5700*, p. 83.

3. See *Likkutei Torah, Bamidbar* 33a.

4. *Me'or Einayim* ibid.

5. *Likkutei Sichot*, vol. 10, p. 23 ff.

6. See *Hayom Yom*, 9 Iyar.

7. Proverbs 10:12.

8. *Negaim* 2:5. See *Likkutei Sichot* ibid., fn. 5; p. 25, fn. 13.

is nothing easier than finding fault with another and nothing harder than recognizing one's own faults.

Therefore, a person should not focus on someone else's flaws, except if he can work with his friend to correct it, but in the main, he must focus on correcting this flaw within himself. A Chasidic saying goes that we were created with two eyes—a right and a left eye: the right one to see the good in another and the left to see any lacking in oneself.[9]

POSITIVE OR NEGATIVE?

"It is hard to have a **positive** life with a **negative** mind."

The correct path in life is to think of the good in another. For it is known that thought is very powerful; it affects a person's surroundings.[10] Therefore, **a person should not think negatively in general and especially about another** because, besides being intrinsically bad in and of itself, it also **affects the world** around the person, including others.[11]

THINK BEFORE YOU THINK

Thought is very powerful. "Thoughts become things," goes the saying.

However, since "the measure of good is so much greater than the measure of not good," by thinking good of another, "G-d will join this thought to actuality,"[12] and the good thought of one person will actually affect the other, revealing the good within him.[13]

9. This is in line with saying: When dealing with others, it is better to use the heart, making every possible allowance. When dealing with oneself, it is better to use the head and take a stricter approach.

10. *Igrot Kodesh by the Lubavitcher Rebbe*, vol. 1, p. 239.

11. See *Likutei Dibburim*, vol. 1, p. 2: Where a person's thoughts are—that is where he is.

12. *Kiddushin* 40a.

13. *Likutei Dibburim*, ibid., p. 3.

40

"לֹא תִקֹּם"

Not to take revenge

"לֹא תִטֹּר"

Not to hold a grudge

We are all one. Just as we would never take revenge or bear a grudge against ourselves, so it should be with another Jew, for we are all part of the same spiritual body. Therefore, these negative emotions should have no place in our hearts. A Jewish heart ought to be pure of such drives. There is another problem with revenge: taking revenge actually means becoming "G-d's policeman," so to speak. This is a denial of the belief that G-d's "justice" can reach every corner of creation.

One who takes revenge against another transgresses a negative commandment, as is stated:[1] "Do not take revenge."

The Talmud[2] explains why a Jew may not take revenge against another Jew. The hand of a person would never take revenge against the other hand that cut it since both belong to the same body, and an individual feels no urge to take revenge against his own body as it is all one entity. It would be nonsensical. So, too, all Jews are part of one "spiritual body," which is the entire Jewish people, and revenge against a different part of the same "body" would similarly be nonsensical.

What is considered revenge? A person says to his friend, "Lend me that object," and his friend does not lend it to him. The next day, his friend comes to borrow from him, and the person says, "I will not lend to you, just as you did not lend to me when I asked you." This is revenge[3] (which is a terribly negative character flaw[4] because the hatred is so deep, it has reached the realm of deed).

So what is the correct way to react in such a case?

When his friend comes to borrow from him, he should be *maavir al midotav*—overcome the desire for retribution and forgive the slight graciously, lending to his friend with a whole heart and not treat the other as he himself was treated.

Ultimately, a person should remember that whatever happens to him was decreed by Heaven, as the Sages

1. Leviticus 19:18
2. Jerusalem Talmud, *Nedarim* 9:4.
3. *Yoma* 23a.
4. *Rambam, Hilchot De'ot* 7:7. (It is noteworthy that this is the only *middah* that *Rambam* refers to as "bad...in the extreme.")

say,[5] "No one bruises his finger below without it having been decreed above"; no man can do to another good or evil except as a messenger of Heaven, and Hashem has many messengers.[6] So the one he is now extracting revenge upon was nothing other than a messenger from Heaven, and thus, revenge is not only forbidden but is also illogical.

Extracting revenge means becoming G-d's "policeman," so to speak. This is a denial of belief in His power. G-d's "justice" reaches every corner of creation (as we say in the morning *Ezrat Avotenu* prayer: "In the heights of the universe is Your dwelling place, and Your judgment and righteousness extend to the ends of the earth"); therefore, **He needs no help to "set the record straight."**

One who bears a grudge against another transgresses a negative commandment (as is stated:[7] "Do not bear a grudge").

What is a grudge? Reuven says to Shimon, "Lend me that thing," and Shimon refuses to lend it to him. The next day, Shimon comes to borrow from Reuven, and Reuven says: "I will lend to you because I'm not like you." This is grudge-bearing.[8]

FORGIVE AND FORGET

Bearing a grudge is very toxic because it is based on an unforgiving and mistaken mindset that says, "When **I** make a mistake, it is because of understandable reasons **outside** of myself; when someone else makes a mistake, it is because there is something wrong with their **essence**." So the fact that I do to another person what they did to me is because of them, because of what they did to me, therefore, it is not really me. However, what they did to me is purely them. This is the polar opposite of *Ahavat Yisrael,* which is the command to love another like "yourself"—**Just as you forgive yourself, forgive the other too.**

---

5. *Chullin* 7b.

6. *Rashi* on Exodus 16:32; *Bamidbar Rabbah* 18:22; *Peleh Yoetz: Emunah*; *Netirah Unetirah.* See *Taanit* 18b.

7. Leviticus 19:18.

8. *Yoma* 23a. See Rashi there, caption: "I am not like you" where he explains that even if one does not say "I am not like you" (or gives an excuse for not lending what the borrower asks for) since the matter is still locked in the heart of the lender, he is guilty of holding a grudge. See *Sefer*

It is less hateful than revenge because no concrete action is taken, however, since Reuven has held that hatred in his heart, even though he takes no actual revenge (i.e., no action) it is nevertheless forbidden. Hatred has absolutely no place in the heart of a Jew. After all, the secrets of the heart are open before G-d.

We need to erase such matters from our hearts,[9] for a Jew's heart should be pure in order to serve Hashem in purity, for the heart is called "the palace of the King,"[10] where we host Hashem (and the Talmud says,[11] "The Merciful One (Hashem) demands the heart"). **It is not fitting that the place in our being where Hashem enters and resides should be corroded and impure with grudges against another Jew and thoughts of revenge.**

Hachinuch, Mitzvah 242.

9. *Rambam, Hilchot De'ot* 7:8.

10. *Orech Apayim* 1:2.

11. *Sanhedrin* 106b.

41

אִסּוּר הַלְבָּנַת פְּנֵי חֲבֵרוֹ—
לְהִמָּנַע מִלְּבַיֵּשׁ אֶת הַזּוּלָת

Not to embarrass another

Shaming another is akin to murder. At the excruciating moment of shame, the tongue accomplishes what a knife can otherwise do. The only difference is that murder is a "one-time" occurrence, while the person shamed is "murdered" each time he recalls his shame.

It is forbidden to shame another either through speech or through action, even a positive action. This is especially so in a public setting and is considered akin to murder.[1]

This prohibition is called "whitening the face of one's fellow in public"[2] because the pain of embarrassment can make a person feel worthless, without G-dly value, thus weakening him and thereby causing the blood to drain from his face, figuratively "**spilling his blood**" and in this way "murdering" him.

THE PAIN OF SHAME

An attack on self-esteem ("invalidation")—at the right moment and in the right way—can last a lifetime.

Shaming someone is, in a way, even worse than murder. Murder is a "one-time" occurrence. However, when a person recalls a shaming experience, the pain is reexperienced, and in this way, the person is being "murdered" each time.

Furthermore, it is such a terrible transgression that the Sages implied that it is even better for a person to sacrifice his life rather than shame another in public (akin to the three cardinal sins[3] of idolatry, forbidden relations, and murder, for which one should give up one's life and be killed if necessary rather than commit any of these sins), as the Sages said,[4] "Better that a

---

1. *Shulchan Aruch Harav* 156:8.

2. Leviticus 19:17, see *Rashi* on the verse. *Avot* 3:11. *Bava Metzia* 58b. *Rambam Hilchot De'ot* 6:8. See *Shulchan Aruch Harav, Hilchot Onaah Ugnevat Daat* 29: "Be extremely careful not to shame anyone of Israel..." (*Kitzur Shulchan Aruch* 29:17). See also *Igrot Kodesh by the Lubavitcher Rebbe*, vol. 16, p. 84: "...shaming another is in most cases caused by the undesirable character trait of anger or pride."

3. According to the opinion of *Tosafot* on *Sotah* 10b. (Others disagree, quoting the terminology *noach lo*... rather than *mechuyav*....)

4. *Sotah* 10b. *Berachot* 43b. Rambam, ibid. (See *Rashi's* explanation to Genesis 38:25.)

person should throw himself into a fiery furnace than whiten someone's face (shame them) in public."

The story is told in the Talmud[5] of Mar Ukva, who secretly supported a poor man in his neighborhood with four *zuzim* (coins) a day without the recipient knowing the identity of his benefactor (Mar Ukva would place the coins in a small hole at the base of the man's front door).

One day, the poor man's inquisitiveness got the better of him and he said to himself, "I would really like to know who is doing this kindness for me."

That day, Mar Ukva walked home late from the study hall with his wife (since a Torah scholar does not walk alone at night) and was spotted by the poor man while placing the coins outside his house.

The poor man followed after them, and when Mar Ukva and his wife realized they were being followed, they fled so as not to embarrass the man with the fact that he, the head of the rabbinical court and a great rabbi of the age, had been supporting him.

The only place they found to hide was in a large, hot oven. Mar Ukva's feet became singed, while his wife's were not. Mar Ukva inferred from this that his merit was smaller than his wife's. His wife said to him: "I am usually at home, where the poor can find me easily, and I give them food, which can be enjoyed immediately. You, however, give them money, which requires work to transform into sustenance. Thus, my merit is greater than yours."

---

5. *Ketubot* 67b.

The Talmud asks, "Why did they need to escape and run into a hot oven?" The Talmud answers, "It is better for one to enter even into a fiery oven than to embarrass his friend in public."[6]

Even a murderer who was (in rare circumstances) sentenced to capital punishment by the Jewish court did not lose his share in the World to Come, while one who embarrassed another in public did indeed lose his share in the World to Come.[7]

6. See *Likkutei Sichot*, vol. 15, p. 135, where a story is quoted concerning R. Shalom DovBer, fifth Lubavitcher Rebbe, when he was still a child and the issue of *halbanat pnei chavero*.

7. *Avot* 3:11.

42

מַרְאִית עַיִן—שֶׁלֹּא לְהִתְנַהֵג בְּצוּרָה שֶׁנִּרְאֵית לֹא רְצוּיָה

Not to act in a way that appears sinful

The Torah instructs us not to do something, however innocent, if it may be construed by others as bad, or "sinful." We are ambassadors of Hashem in this world, and it is not fitting to be even "suspected" of wrongdoing. Thus, before doing something, it is important to reflect how the action we wish to take will appear in the eyes of others.

Not only must we be careful not to sin, of course, but we must also be careful not to do anything that an observer may "**suspect**" to be sinful, for this is also not fitting for a Jew.

This is what is called *marit ayin*—the semblance, or appearance, to the eye of the onlooker, i.e., doing something that could be interpreted by an onlooker as sinful, even though there may be an innocent explanation for it. This could cause an onlooker to mistakenly think that what he believed to be prohibited is permitted or to think of the perpetrator as sinful.

Therefore, the Sages forbade many things in order that others should not suspect a person of committing a transgression, the rationale being that it is necessary for a Jew to keep far from sin to the extent that he is not even suspected of it.

This concept was taken into account in the *Beit Hamikdash*.[1] All of the coins that were donated were collected in a certain chamber. Three times a year, a Kohen would enter the chamber to fill three large boxes with coins, from which the communal offerings and other necessities were purchased. The Kohen who would gather the money would enter wearing a garment specifically made without pockets or hems so that no one would suspect him of hiding money.

This practice was enacted because of the requirement to be innocent in the eyes of others, as much as one needs to be innocent before Hashem, as is stated,[2] "And you will be vindicated before G-d and man." And

1. *Shekalim* 3:2.

2. Numbers 32:22.

it is also said,[3] "And you will find favor and good understanding in the eyes of G-d and man."

If it happens that a person is suspected of something negative, that itself may well be a sign that the very thing he is suspected of is indeed to be found within himself, and it was brought to his attention through the suspicion of others in order that he may eradicate it.

This is borne out by a teaching of the Talmud that says,[4] "A person would not be suspected of something negative unless he had once done that thing. If he did not do all of it, then he did part of it. If he did not do part of it, then he thought in his heart about doing it. If he did not think about doing it, then he must have seen others do it and was happy."

So being suspected of something negative is not to be taken lightly. In order to avoid this, a person must endeavor to be viewed as trustworthy and acceptable to others[5] by behaving in a way that will be considered a *Kiddush Hashem*—sanctification of Hashem's name (as explained in section 11)—**because every Jew is an ambassador of Hashem in this world.**

3. Proverbs 3:4.

4. *Moed Katan* 18b.

5. *Shekalim*, ibid. *Rambam, Hilchot Shekalim* 2:10. See *Kitzur Shulchan Aruch* 29:20.

43

אִסּוּר גְּנֵבָה וּגְזֵלָה

The prohibition against theft and robbery

Taking what is not ours, however small the amount and however insignificant the object, is tantamount to taking the life of the victim. Hashem gives each one of us exactly what we need to fulfill our purpose in life. If even a hairbreadth is missing from the resources allocated to one person because it was stolen by another, it makes it impossible for the victim to fulfill their purpose to perfection, leaving his life incomplete.

It is forbidden to steal (to take for oneself the money or possessions of another person in secret, without their knowing), which is called *genevah*, or to rob (to take something from another openly by force), which is called *gezelah*, as the verse says,[1] "You shall not steal...and you shall not rob." This applies even to things of little value. (There is no small-claims court in Jewish law).

Theft and robbery are forbidden even if the culprit had in mind to return what was stolen, or even if he only stole in jest, or even if was willing to repay the owner more than the worth of the object.[2]

Theft and robbery have very harmful ramifications for both the **thief** as well as the **victim.**

Concerning the victim, the Talmud says,[3] "Whoever steals a penny from his fellow, it is as if he has taken his life."

This is because every individual has an essential connection to his possessions since the Holy One, blessed is He, gives each individual what he requires to fulfill his purpose in life, and the thief has therefore deprived the victim of the ability to fulfill his purpose. In this way, the thief has taken the life of the victim.

And concerning the thief, his actions damage him greatly by blemishing his faith and connection to Hashem.

---

1. Leviticus 19:11-13.

2. *Bava Metzia* 61b. *Shulchan Aruch, Choshen Mishpat* 359:2. *Shulchan Aruch Harav, Hilchot Gezelah Ugenevah* 1-3. (However, when in danger a person may save his life with the money of his friend, provided his intention is to repay. Should this not be the case, then it would be forbidden to use one's friend's money even to save oneself because "whoever steals from his friend even a *shaveh prutah*—the smallest amount—it is considered as if he took his soul" (*Bava Kama* 119a).)

3. *Bava Kama* ibid.

For, the foundation of our faith is that Hashem feeds and sustains every one of us and gives us what we require to fulfill our purpose in a manner permitted by the Torah, without having to resort to theft. By stealing, the thief shows that he does not believe this; rather, he thinks that Hashem is deficient and needs the thief's "help," as it were, in order to fulfill his personal needs.

Thus, stealing is more than a Torah prohibition; it is a statement of nonbelief in G-d as an active force in the world. (Perhaps that is why the Talmud tells us[4] that the very first question a person will be asked by the Heavenly court after leaving this world will be *"Did you deal honestly in business?"*)

And this is aside from the fact that it is impossible to benefit through theft and to acquire one penny more than what Hashem has decreed for a person to receive, as the Sages say,[5] "No one can touch what is prepared for his fellow...by even a hairsbreadth." For what a person will earn is fixed on Rosh Hashanah[6] and no machinations of someone else, or for that matter the person himself, will change that one iota.

Even though both of these transgressions, theft and robbery, each represent a breach in one's faith in Hashem, there is nevertheless a large difference between them.

NO ONE CAN TOUCH WHAT IS DESTINED FOR ANOTHER EVEN BY A HAIRSBREADTH (TALMUD)

It is explained that the Talmud's use of the term "hairsbreadth" is intentional, for it is an analogy to man's livelihood, and in this way, the Sages are teaching us a most valuable lesson. If Hashem designed each hair to have its own follicle from which it grows and from which it receives its nuture, with no two hairs sharing the same follicle, then we can understand that certainly each person also has his own source of livelihood in Heaven, and no one else can usurp it.

---

4. *Shabbat* 31a.

5. *Yoma* 38b. Jerusalem Talmud, *Yoma* 3:9.

6. *Beitzah* 16a.

Thieves (who steal secretly) must repay, according to the Torah, two (in some cases four or five) times the value of their theft in fines, whereas robbers (who steal openly) do not.

The rationale behind this is because the thief has not only stolen but has exhibited a lack of faith that is worse than the robber's. The thief steals at night because he is afraid of man; therefore, he steals secretly. However, he is not afraid of G-d, Who commanded us not to steal. The thief thus places man higher than G-d and is therefore in need of greater rectification and is punished more severely than the robber who steals openly by threat of violence, indicating that he fears neither G-d nor man.[7]

We see[8] concerning theft (and robbery) that they share a severe and unique characteristic. Both are not seen as a "one-time" deed; rather, theft (and robbery) are considered "continuous" acts.

That is, every moment that the stolen property is not returned (insofar as it is the property of the victim but is being held forcibly in the possession of the thief), it is considered as if it is being stolen anew every instant.[9]

---

7. *Bava Kama* 79b. See *Likkutei Sichot*, vol. 16, p. 260.

8. *Likkutei Sichot*, vol. 17, p. 209.

9. The reason for this is because the location of the property in the thief's domain is the essence of theft and contradicts its true and intended status, which is to be in the possession of the rightful owner.

44

אִסּוּר גְּנֵבַת דַּעַת—שֶׁלֹּא לְהַטְעוֹת אוֹ לְרַמּוֹת

The prohibition against deception

Far worse than stealing someone's material possessions or money is the theft of their most precious possession—their mind. This is exactly what happens when we are misled, deceived, or lied to.

There is a form of theft that does not involve stealing physical possessions or money but is worse.[1]

This is the theft of "spiritual property," so to speak—**the theft of a person's mind**, or knowledge (which is a person's most valuable possession), and is referred to in the Torah as *genevat daat*—the theft of knowledge,[2] which is deception of the highest order, because it harms the person, not his money, and is included in the transgression, "You shall not steal."[3]

The Sages said,[4] "There are seven thieves, and chief among them is one who deceives others."

This prohibition of deception forbids misleading another person. For example, making a statement that may be technically correct but is intended to leave a false impression.

If a seller knows of a fault with the merchandise he is selling that is not apparent to the eye, he is obligated to inform the buyer.

Even to cause a person to think he has been done a favor, when in reality, he has not, is deception and is forbidden.

For example: It is forbidden to give another an invitation or gift knowing that it will not be accepted, and the donor is doing so only to give the impression that he likes the recipient, when in actuality, this is not the case.

---

1. *Shaarei Teshuvah L'Rabbenu Yonah* §184.

2. See *Rashi* on Genesis 31:26.

3. *Chullin* 94a. *Rambam, Hilchot De'ot* 2:6. *Tur* and *Shulchan Aruch, Choshen Mishpat* 228:6. *Shulchan Aruch Harav, Hilchot Onaah Ugenevat Daat*, 12-14. See *Encyclopedia Talmudit*, vol. 6: *Genevat Daat*, p. 225.

4. *Tosefta, Bava Kama* 7:3.

Even worse is he who works to know his friends' secrets through deception—this too is considered "theft of knowledge."[5]

Also included in this category is flattery, that is, displaying false affection for a person that is not felt in your heart, as is explained in section 47. This is not only theft of another's mind but it is theft of his heart too.

Besides the harm that deception can cause to another person, it also harms the deceiver, who thinks that G-d is defective and needs help to run the world, just as the thief thinks, as explained in section 43. So the deceiver manipulates others into doing or thinking what the deceiver wants but which may not be in the best interest of the one being deceived.

In truth, deception does not achieve anything. It is totally unnecessary, for G-d runs the world with justice, righteousness, and truth. **So deceiving, exploiting, or manipulating others for one's own ends, besides being the greatest theft, is also pointless.**

Rather, the way of a Jew should be to conduct oneself with honesty, openness, and *temimut*—sincerity.

5. See *Peleh Yo'etz*: *Genevah* and *Dibbur* (stealing the mind of one's friend).

45

"לֹא תַחְמֹד" וְ"לֹא תִתְאַוֶּה"

The prohibition against desiring the possessions of another

What is destined for one person to receive is not destined for another. Desiring what another person has is therefore a complete breakdown of belief in Hashem's ability to judge correctly what is fitting for each one to receive in life.

The laws of society that we live by are based on "external" values. They have nothing to do with our inner essence. Societ considers what we do to matter, so how we affect one another is governed by law. However, society has nothing to say about "internal" values, what goes on inside a person—for this, society does not legislate.

However, this is not the Torah system. For a Jew, not only what one does matters, but what one feels in the heart matters.

We see this from the Ten Commandments. It is written in the Ten Commandments as they appear in the portion of *Yitro*:[1] *Lo tachmod*—"Do not covet," and in the Ten Commandments as they appear in the portion of *Va'etchanan*:[2] *Lo titaveh*—"Do not desire." These are not two phrases for one concept but rather two phrases for two concepts:

"Do not covet" means do not do anything, i.e., take action, to acquire the possessions of someone when he does not want to sell, even offering to pay full price for them.

"Do not desire" refers to not desiring another's possessions, even in your heart. Since matters of the heart are revealed before Hashem, therefore, **the Torah legislates even for matters of the heart.**

From the fact that two phrases, i.e., "Do not desire" and "Do not covet," are used for one commandment, we learn that one who desires will eventually covet (and try to acquire the object of his desire). And once he covets, he will eventually steal, as we learn from the

---

1. Exodus 20:14.

2. Deuteronomy 5:18.

verse, "And he coveted the fields and robbed them,"[3] teaching us that **coveting ends in theft.**

The commentators explain[4] that since the commands "Do not covet" and "Do not desire" are the last of the Ten Commandments, they include all ten, thus indicating their importance (because through desiring and coveting, a person could come to sin in many other matters, for most sins come from greed).

In general, desiring what another has is the result of lack of belief in Hashem. Each person receives from Hashem exactly what he needs and when he needs it, so that each one of us can fulfill the purpose for which we were brought into this world.

Consequently, what is destined for one person to receive is not destined for another and desiring what the other has implies that a person believes G-d to be deficient in His understanding of our needs and that we have a better understanding—a sure recipe for failure and unhappiness.

3. Micah 2:2. (See II Kings 21 concerning the story of Achav and Navot.)

4. See *Sefer Hachinuch, Mitzvah 416* and that which is explained in *Peleh Yo'etz: Chemdah*. See *Shulchan Aruch, Choshen Mishpat* §359.

46

אוֹנָאָה וְרַמָּאוּת

The prohibition against causing pain to another by verbal deceit, hurting another's feelings, or cheating

---

Just as the Torah instructs us not to mislead another person in business and financial matters, however small the deception, so, too, and even more so, in any personal interaction, we are instructed never to deceive or hurt another with words.

The Torah commands us,[1] "You shall not hurt the feelings of one another...for I am Hashem your G-d."

It is therefore forbidden to hurt a fellow Jew in any way, certainly not to deceive or cheat another. Even verbally, speaking abusively to another, thus causing him harm or pain, is totally forbidden.

This applies not just in business matters but to all interpersonal relationships.[2]

Therefore, just as we are forbidden to cheat or deceive in our business dealings, so, too, and even more so, we are forbidden to deceive or hurt with words, even if true. The Torah calls verbal abuse and deception *onaat devarim*.[2]

What is verbal deception? For example, one is not allowed to ask a seller: "How much does this item cost?" if one does not intend to purchase it or does not have the money to do so. In this situation, one is misleading the seller, and by not purchasing the item, the seller will realize the deception and be pained by it.

Another example: one is not allowed to say to one who has repented, "Remember your old ways!"

Similarly, one is not allowed to tell someone who is the child of converts, "Remember what your parents did!"

Furthermore, one is not allowed to say something that will reveal the flaws of one's friend, such as asking an individual known to be ignorant on a certain subject,

1. Leviticus 25:17.

2. See Rashi there. *Bava Metzia* 4:10. *Tur* and *Shulchan Aruch Choshen Mishpat* 228:1. *Shulchan Aruch Harav, Hilchot Onaah Ugenevat Daat,* 27 ff. Also see *Hayom Yom*, 27 Sivan.

"What is your response on this matter?" or "What is your opinion on this topic?"[3]

One must also not speak of something in front of another that will embarrass that person.[4]

The same applies to all such matters that would cause pain to the heart of another.[5] (When in doubt, a good rule to follow would be to ask oneself before saying something that may possibly cause another pain or embarrassment to another: "What I am about to say—**is it true, is it kind (or will it cause pain), and is it necessary?**")

It is even forbidden to call someone by a nickname, even if the person does not become embarrassed by the nickname, but you merely *intend* to embarrass them.

All of this is in the category of forbidden harmful statements and verbal deception.[6]

Verbal deception is a more serious transgression than cheating in business since the latter can be repaid, whereas the former cannot, and the latter merely harms someone else's possessions, whereas the former harms the person himself.

One who cries out to Hashem due to the pain of verbal deception is answered immediately since it pains the heart and can easily bring forth tears,[7] as the Talmud says,[8] "All the Heavenly gates are locked, except

3. *Shulchan Aruch Harav* ibid., 28 et al. (See *Peleh Yo'etz*: *Onaah*.)

4. *Shulchan Aruch Harav* ibid., 29.

5. Ibid., 27, 28.

6. Ibid., 29.

7. Ibid., 27.

8. *Bava Metzia* 59a. See *Hayom Yom*, ibid.

for the gate of *onaah*." The gates of Heaven are always open for one who cries out from the pain of *onaah*.

47

חֲנוּפָה

Flattery

False flattery and insincere praise are not just inappropriate for a Jew, but the Torah actually forbids them. What we feel in our heart and what we say with our mouth should always be aligned so that we act with sincerity at all times.

Flattery (insincere praise that has an ulterior motive, as opposed to real praise that is sincere) is viewed by the Sages as deception. An individual who praises or shows fondness for someone else, but does not feel that way in his heart, is guilty of *chanifah*—flattery, which is forbidden.[1] It shows lack of sincerity and is inappropriate behavior.

There is another, worse, form of *chanifah*: telling a sinner that he is righteous and what he is doing is right, rather than rebuking him.[2]

This is a *chillul Hashem*—a desecration of G-d's name that falsifies the Torah, encourages the performance of wrong deeds, and shows that the flatterer is more concerned not to offend the sinner than he cares about G-d's will.

The Talmud has a very negative view of flatterers and says about them,[3] "Four types of people never merit Hashem's presence: scoffers, flatterers, liars, and slanderers."

To show just how serious this prohibition is, the Talmud shares with us the following episode that took place shortly before the destruction of the second *Beit Hamikdash*:[4]

The king at that time was Agrippa (a grandchild of Herod), who was an excellent ruler and highly respectful of the Sages and the Torah. However, calling himself "king" over the Jewish people violated Jewish law, for he was descended from gentile slaves, and the

---

1. See *Encyclopedia Talmudit*, vol. 16: *Chanifah*.

2. See *Sefer Peleh Yoetz: Chanifah*.

3. *Sotah* 42a. See also 41b there.

4. Ibid. 41a.

Torah states,[5] "You may not place over yourselves a gentile who is not your brother."

Agrippa realized that he was not permitted to be king during the *mitzvah* of *Hakhel*, which took place once every seven years, when the king would read aloud from the Torah in the Temple courtyard in the presence of all the people. Agrippa reached the verse "You may not place over yourselves a gentile who is not your brother" and began to weep (for this verse disqualified him from being the king).

At that moment, the Sages and the people comforted him, saying, "Don't worry, Agrippa. You are our brother. You are our brother," thus approving his reign, in violation of the Torah. Although under the circumstances, the Sages were in no position to admonish him, nevertheless, they should have remained silent, which would have been understood as respectful disapproval.

The Talmud says[6] that whoever flatters a sinner will eventually "fall into his hand" (a fitting consequence on the scale of "measure for measure"). Furthermore, any community that flatters sinners will eventually be driven into exile.[7] Unfortunately, many negative consequences occurred to the nation as a result of this event.

In any case, insincere flattery never achieves its desired goal. On the

INSINCERE FLATTERY ACHIEVES THE OPPOSITE OF WHAT IS INTENDED

This is so not only between man and man but applies even to the Jewish people as a whole. Over the course of history, it can be seen that the veneration (and imitation) of the host or majority culture by the Jewish community of the time (being the highest form of flattery) has likewise invariably ended in tragedy. The hallmark of the Jewish people

5. Deuteronomy 17:15.

6. *Sotah* 41b.

7. Ibid. 42a.

contrary, the Sages taught that only "words that come from the heart enter the heart."[8]

The correct path in life is one governed by the following principle: Always act with *temimut*—sincerity—with the **mouth and heart aligned** so that one's inner character and the outer manifestation of that character match.

(There are, however, three cases where the first type of flattery is permitted:[9]

(a) for the sake of peace at home with one's spouse;

(b) in order to learn Torah from one's teacher;

(c) to minimize disputes.)

has always been its independent spiritual identity. Abandonment of this honored status by taking on a foreign identity through assimilation within the majority culture has never led to the desired acceptance. On the contrary, such episodes have been one of the causes that led to empowerment of the host culture in the persecution of the Jewish minority.

8. Based on Proverbs 27:19 (see *Metzudat David*) according to many opinions. See *Berachot* 6b. Quoted by R. Moshe Ibn Ezra, *Shirat Yisrael*, p. 156. Other sources explain that Moses was able to transmit the entire Torah to the Jewish people, as recorded in Deuteronomy, in just thirty-seven days, because the words he spoke came from his heart. This is alluded to in the fact that the numerical value of "the heart" (*halev*) is also thirty-seven.

9. See sources cited in *Encyclopedia Talmudit*, ibid.

48

הָאִסּוּר לְהַזִּיק אוֹ לִגְרוֹם הֶזֵּק לְמָמוֹן שֶׁל חֲבֵרוֹ

The prohibition against damaging or causing damage to another's property

---

Just as the Torah forbids stealing or robbing from another person, so too are we forbidden to damage, or even to cause damage, to another person's property. In short, one should never be a "damager." Even inadvertent damage that we may have caused should bring us concern that we came to be the "agent" through which harm came to another.

Just as it is forbidden to steal or rob, even with the intention of returning what was taken, so is it forbidden to damage another person's property, whether directly or even indirectly (by causing the damage), and this is so even if the guilty party intends to pay for the damage.[1]

Simply put, a Jew should never be a "damager" (neither physically nor spiritually).

On the contrary, one should always look to be of help and benefit to another (as R. Yosef Yitzchak, sixth Lubavitcher Rebbe, said: **"When two meet, a third should benefit,"** meaning that besides any common benefit that two people can create, or share, from their meeting, they should see to it that benefit should accrue to a third person).[2]

If one did cause damage, even inadvertently, to someone else, this requires introspection on our part: "How come I became the instrument through which damage was caused to another?"[3]

---

1. *Shulchan Aruch Harav, Hilchot Nizkei Mammon*, 1 (and see there, 5). (However, if one intends to pay back with something better, then it could be argued that it would not be forbidden. See *Likkutei Sichot*, vol. 34, p. 52, quoted in *Shulchan Menachem*, vol. 7, p. 131.)

2. Quoted in *Igrot Kodesh by the Lubavitcher Rebbe*, vol. 8, p. 190.

3. See *Rashi* on Exodus 21:13. (In his comment, *Rashi* quotes the verse from I Samuel (24:14): "From the wicked comes forth wickedness." Conversely, in Proverbs (12:21) it says: "No transgression will occur to (or come about through) a righteous person."

49

הָאִסּוּר לְהַכּוֹת אֶת חֲבֵרוֹ

The prohibition against striking one's fellow

Each person is made in the image of G-d. Striking, or raising a hand to strike another, in anger is the ultimate denial of the manifestation of Hashem's presence in this world.

It is forbidden by the Torah to physically strike another Jew (G-d forbid).[1]

This is true even if the other gives permission because the body does not belong to a person[2] to strike, damage, or disrespect in any way. Having been made in the image of Hashem, it is only "on loan" from Hashem to be used for His service[3] but is not the personal property of anyone.

Even if someone only raises his hand but does not actually strike another, this is a transgression (against Hashem), and one who does this is considered wicked.[4]

The reason why even (merely) raising a hand against another person is sinful, it is explained,[5] is because the purpose of man's creation is "to serve his Creator"[6] by fulfilling the Torah and the *mitzvot* with every organ and limb of his body.

Man was given hands in order to give,[7] to express kindness to his fellow man—"the hand which distributes righteousness."[8]

Therefore, when a person raises his hand against his friend, it is also a transgression against Hashem, because he is using the hand that Hashem has given him for the opposite of its true purpose.

For this reason, such a person has sinned against G-d

---

1. See *Rambam, Hilchot Chovel Umazik* 5:1. *Shulchan Aruch, Choshen Mishpat* 420:1.

2. *Shulchan Aruch Harav, Hilchot Nizkei Guf Venefesh,* 4. See *Likkutei Sichot,* vol. 34, p. 106.

3. And not for self-indulgence (See the opening chapters of *Kuntres Umaayan* and numerous other sources).

4. See *Rashi* on Exodus 2:13. *Sanhedrin* 58b. *Rambam* ibid., *halachah* 2.

5. *Likkutei Sichot,* vol. 31, p. 5.

6. *Mishnah* and *Baraita* end of *Kiddushin.*

7. See *Likkutei Sichot* ibid.

8. As expressed in the *Tanya,* ch. 23.

as well as acted wickedly against his fellow man. And this misuse of the hand begins even when it is just raised (threateningly), even before he has actually struck his friend (G-d forbid).

50

"לִפְנֵי עִוֵּר לֹא תִתֵּן מִכְשׁוֹל"

Not to place an obstacle before the blind

The blind are vulnerable and dependent upon the guidance of others. The Torah forbids placing, or even failing to remove, an obstacle in the path of the blind. The term blind," in the Torah refers not only to one unable to see physically but includes those who are "blind" in other ways, being naïve or unknowing in a specific matter and thus susceptible to the wrong guidance and advice. The Torah is concerned for their welfare and warns against misguiding such people.

It is written in the Torah,[1] "Do not place a stumbling block before the blind."

The Sages tell us that the term "blind" in the verse refers not only to the physically unseeing (it is forbidden to create or leave an obstacle that will cause the "blind" to trip up, and one is required to remove obstacles from their path); this verse also applies to those who are "blind" in other ways, being naïve or unknowing in a specific matter and thus susceptible to the wrong guidance and advice.[2] To cause such people to "trip up" is forbidden.

Thus, it is forbidden to entrap another into violating a Torah command (G-d forbid), for example, to serve nonkosher food even to a Jew who does not keep the Torah and the *mitzvot*.[3]

Also included in this commandment is a ban on knowingly giving another bad advice. When giving advice, we need to have in mind only the good of the one asking.[4]

Furthermore, it is explained[5] that we may not even give good advice to the "blind" person in a certain matter if it is self-serving advice, even if it will cause no loss to the recipient of the advice.

This is considered to be placing an obstacle before the blind since at the time we gave the advice, we were

1. Leviticus 19:14.

2. See *Rashi* there.

3. *Torat Kohanim*. See *Pesachim* 22b; *Shulchan Aruch Harav*, *Orach Chaim* 163:2; 347:3, 4, and 5; 524:12; 526:5. (See *Tosafot* on *Shabbat* 3a, caption: *Bava d'reisha*.)

4. See *Rashi* on Leviticus ibid. (It is explained elsewhere that the prohibition of not placing a stumbling block before the blind applies also to oneself, in a spiritual sense, when dealing with the *yetzer hara*, which "blinds" us to the truth and in this way opens us to its enticement. In such a case, it is easy to give oneself, so to speak, "bad advice.")

5. *Likkutei Sichot*, vol. 27, p. 141 ff.

only considering ourselves and not the good of the other (the stumbling block in this case is not the advice, rather the way it is given).

We can learn from this last point an important lesson in *Ahavat Yisrael*, that when doing a favor for another, it is not enough that the end result should be good, but even the intent and the purpose should be for the good of the other person.

51

הֲשָׁבַת אֲבֵדָה

The requirement to return lost objects

There is an essential connection between people and their possessions because these possessions are the resources and the raw material with which each of us fulfills our mission in this world. For this reason, should we find a lost article, the Torah commands us to seek out its owner in order to return it to them. In Judaism, this is not considered a virtuous deed of high morality as does society. For us, it is a self-understood norm so that the divine plan for creation may reach its fulfillment.

Someone who returns a lost object that is of great value is considered by society to be a person of unusually high moral caliber, who should receive some type of reward for acting above and beyond the norm.

The Torah, however, considers this to be the common and expected norm and teaches us that if we come across a lost article, we are obliged to seek out the owner in order to return it (as is stated,[1] "You should return them to your brother").

(Although from the strict standpoint of the law, we are not obligated to return the lost object of a non-Jewish person, nevertheless, if not returning it will cause a desecration of G-d's name, we are obliged to take the trouble to find the owner and return it.[2] Furthermore, if returning it will bring about a *Kiddush Hashem*—"sanctification of G-d's name"—then it is praiseworthy to go to the effort to do so, as in the classic story quoted in the Jerusalem Talmud[3] concerning R. Shimon ben Shetach, cited in section 11.)

The Talmud says[4] that there are three categories of people whom G-d praises from Heaven each day. One of them is a poor person who returns a found object. Rambam rules that he who picks up a lost object but does not return it is excluded from doing repentance since it is impossible to repent if you don't know against whom you have sinned.[5]

---

1. Deuteronomy 22:1.

2. *Shulchan Aruch Harav, Hilchot Metziah Upikadon*, 38.

3. Jerusalem Talmud, *Bava Metzia* 2:5.

4. *Pesachim* 113a.

5. If one finds a lost article and does not know to whom it belongs, a question should be asked to a competent halachic authority, for there are circumstances when it is necessary to to announce or advertise the found object and hold it until the owner comes to collect it and there are circumstances when the finder may keep the object.

The inner rationale behind this *mitzvah* of returning lost objects is that there is an essential connection between a person and his possessions. Before a person's soul descends to this world, it is entrusted with a specific mission, and all the resources needed to fulfill that purpose are prepared by Hashem so that they are ready to be used in achieving that goal.

Thus, it is a *mitzvah* to return a lost object to its owner so that he can thereby fulfill his purpose to perfection.[6]

The *mitzvah* of "returning of a lost object" applies also in a "**spiritual**" sense[7]—if one sees a Jew who is "**lost**" from the way of Judaism (G-d forbid). In addition to the obligation that stems from the *mitzvah* of *Ahavat Yisrael* and also of guiding a person away from negativity, it is a *mitzvah* to draw another Jew closer to his heritage and return him to Torah and *mitzvot*, **thereby returning this, the most precious of all "lost objects," to its "Owner," the Holy one, blessed is He** (as is explained in section 32).

---

6. It could be said that not seeking out the owner of a lost article is akin to "spiritual" murder since the true owner can no longer completely fullfull his purpose in life.

7. *Likkutei Sichot*, vol. 1, p. 103 (the saying of the Sages (*Chagigah* 4a) is elucidated there: *Eizeh hu shoteh*—"Who is a fool?" (fool referring to the *yetzer hara*, the old foolish King) *Hame'abeid kol "mah" shenosnim lo*—"he who loses everything" (the fool loses the "*mah*," which refers to the soul, the power to be nullified to G-dliness and in this way be connected to Hashem).

PART FOUR

Our Relationship with the World

52

שְׁמִירָה מִפְּנֵי סַכָּנָה

Avoiding danger

The Torah does not permit us to knowingly put ourselves in danger. We don't rely on miracles because it is not good that G-d should have to change nature just for us.

It is forbidden to place oneself or another in danger, for example, to stand in a dangerous place, such as near an unstable wall that might fall, as is written:[1] "You shall guard yourselves very carefully" and also[2] "...make sure to guard yourselves and your souls well."

The Sages say,[3] "Danger is more severe than transgression." Therefore, since the spiritual power, whose job is to be an accuser (Satan), seizes upon moments when we are in danger,[4] we ought to keep away from places and situations of danger, for we have a principle that "we do not rely on miracles."[5]

The reason for this is because Hashem desires that the natural order of things—what is usual and customary—should continue as much as possible without overt intercession on His part so that our free choice may continue to operate. Nature is precious in His eyes; it's the system that He created and introduced into the world for it to function, and He only abrogates it when absolutely necessary—"G-d does not perform a miracle without good reason."[6]

In any case, a person can never know if his own merits are sufficient to warrant a miracle, especially for

1. Deuteronomy 4:15.

2. Supra fn. 1 verse 9.

3. *Chulin* 10a.

4. See *Menachot* 36a.

5. See *Pesachim* 64b.

6. See *Likkutei Sichot*, vol. 13, pp. 39-40 and fn. 6 (where the exposition of *Ran* on this topic is mentioned). See also *Shabbat* 53b: "The Rabbis taught...how inferior is this man for whom the order of creation was changed" (by the performance of a miracle). It is explained that the rationale behind this is because material things are G-d's "vessels" (*Likkutei Sichot*, vol. 10, pp. 4-5) and He wants them to be used in His service so that the physical be made holy. Therefore, we are responsible to do whatever possible to reveal Hashem within nature, using the natural order of things, so that there is no need for Hashem to perform a supernatural miracle outside of nature on our behalf. See *Shabbat* 32a; *Taanit* 20b; *Likkutei Sichot*, vol. 5, p. 396.

himself. And if he does warrant such an occurrence, it is a cause for concern as it may lessen any accumulated merits that are to his credit, which were called upon to warrant the miracle on his behalf.[7]

7. See previous fn.

53

בַּל תַּשְׁחִית—הָאִסּוּר לְאַבֵּד לָרִיק וּלְהַשְׁחִית

Not to be wasteful

The Torah forbids unnecessary waste. The resources of this world contain “sparks” of holy energy that await elevation and redemption from “exile“ within the physical. This is accomplished through their proper use as was intended by Hashem. Unnecessary waste loses the owner the opportunity to elevate these sparks, which are now “lost” in exile, leaving the life-mission of this person incomplete.

The Torah commanded[1] the Jewish people entering the Land of Israel that if they would need to besiege a city, they should not cause excess destruction, specifically not to destroy its (fruit-bearing) trees.

The Sages of the Talmud reasoned[2] that this principle goes beyond war and fruit trees: If in the extreme case of war (one of conquest), when destruction is the norm, it is forbidden to cut down trees so as not to destroy or waste things useful to the world, then how much more so does this apply in the normal course of life.

This general principle is the *mitzvah* of *bal tashchit*—the prohibition not to destroy anything that may be of use to people.

Therefore, it is forbidden to break vessels, tear clothing, or throw away or ruin food unnecessarily. This is considered wasteful, and in doing so, one transgresses this negative commandment of *bal tashchit*—not to waste anything useful. (Obviously, if it is for some constructive purpose, then it is permitted.)

The inner rationale behind this *mitzvah*, it is explained,[3] is that when we wear, eat, or use material things of this world, we are coming into contact with the life-force (the "sparks of holiness") contained within these things.

This life-force is associated specifically with the source of the user's soul—it has been earmarked in Heaven

---

1. Deuteronomy 20:19-20.

2. By *kal v'chomer*. See *Shulchan Aruch Harav, Hilchot Shemirat Guf Venefesh Ubal Tashchit*, 14. Based on *Mishneh Lemelech's* explanation of *Shabbat* 129a; *Kiddushin* 32a. (See also *Shabbat* 105b; *Bava Kama* 91a.)

3. *Keter Shem Tov* §218. See *Likkutei Sichot*, vol. 3, p. 824; vol. 21, p. 80.

for his use in order that he may "elevate" these "sparks" through his use of them in serving Hashem.

In this way, each person fulfills his purpose and ultimately the purpose of the entire creation, which is to use the physical to serve G-d, as the Sages say, "G-d desired to have a dwelling place in the lower worlds," in this way elevating the life-force (the "sparks of holiness") within the physical to holiness.[4]

This, taught the Baal Shem Tov, is the inner meaning of the saying of our Sages[5] "The Torah cares about the money of the Jewish people" because within that money are contained sparks of holiness that await elevation and "redemption" from "exile" within the physical. **By unnecessarily wasting physical things, not only is the owner of these resources losing his opportunity to elevate these sparks of holiness, but the sparks themselves are now "lost" in "exile."**

Thus, G-d sees the great Divine potential in the existence of the world and in material things. For this reason, virtuous people also delight in the preservation of the world and will respect material things for their use in serving Hashem.

Perhaps the greatest waste a person can be guilty of is the waste of our G-d-given talents for ends not germane to our purpose and goal in life.

---

4. See *Tanya*, ch 37.

5. *Rosh Hashanah* 27a.

54

הַצֹּרֶךְ לְהִתְחַבֵּר עִם אֲנָשִׁים טוֹבִים וּרְאוּיִים

The necessity to associate with righteous people

The community we live in and the friends we associate with affect us deeply, not only socially and materially but emotionally and spiritually as well. Choosing the right "environment" is one of life's most impactful decisions.

People are greatly influenced by the "social" environment within which they live and especially by their "spiritual" environment. These play a large part in molding a person's character and outlook in life.

Indeed, it is explained,[1] that a person's associates and neighbors affect the person not only outwardly, in matters of behavior, but their influence can reach deep within a person, affecting one's inner essence.[2]

In this vein, Rambam[3] writes that it is human nature to be drawn after the opinions and actions of our friends and acquaintances. This can be positive in the right environment but negative in the wrong environment.

This negativity stems from the fact that society often accepts certain "norms" and behaviors as normal and acceptable only because a lot of people behave that way, whereas in truth, these behaviors and attitudes could be intrinsically immoral or wrong.

The Torah's moral compass of absolute values gives us a clear guide: not everything accepted as "normal" in society is indeed so. **Society tends to confuse two terms: that which is "average" with that which is "normal."** Just because the **"average"** person does something (how often do we hear "...but everyone does it...all my friends do it") doesn't make it right, moral, or **"normal."** What society accepts as the "average" is often rationalized into the "normal" in a subtle, subliminal way, when in fact, it could be far from what the Torah teaches us is the true norm.

---

1. *Likkutei Sichot*, vol. 19, p. 62.
2. See *Bava Batra* 109b, on the difference between the offspring of Moses and Aaron.
3. *Hilchot De'ot* 6:1.

Therefore, choosing the right environment is one of life's great decisions.

For this reason, one should always choose the company of good friends and try to live in a place that can exert a positive spiritual influence (and this could be by being the one to create the positive climate oneself. This is especially so in the case of those who go to live in a place specifically to elevate the environment—*shlichut*—thus lighting the way for others.[4] In such a case, an additional principle applies, that **"as long as one is giving to others, one does not absorb from the environment"**).[5]

THE LAMPLIGHTER

"A Chasid is a lamplighter, one who puts his own affairs aside and sets out to light up the souls of others with the light of Torah and *mitzvot*."

Stories are told in the *Chumash* and the Talmud regarding the great impact, both positive and negative, of one's friends.

For example, in the desert, the tribes of Yehudah, Yissachar, and Zevulun camped near Moshe, who studied Torah, and this affected them. Each of these tribes became great in Torah knowledge because of the principle,[6] "The righteous do good, and this projects itself to his neighbor."

However, the tribe of Reuven, which camped close to Korach, were caught up in his dispute because of the principle, "The wicked do bad, and this affects his neighbor."

---

4. See *Sefer Hasichot 5701*, p. 136. *Torat Menachem—Hitvaaduyot*, vol, 34, p. 129 ff. Such "lamplighters" are accompanied by the promise that "a little light dispels much darkness."

5. This principle is quoted numerous times in the Talmud, *Rambam*, and *Shulchan Aruch*. Specifically see *Chullin* 8b, *Tosafot*, caption: *Sakin*; ibid., 112b, *Rashi*, caption: *Imlach*. *Rambam*, *Hilchot Ma'achalot Asurot* 17:3. *Shulchan Aruch*, *Yoreh De'ah* 1:70 and numerous further instances.

6. *Negaim* 12:6. *Sukkah* 56b.

The Talmud[7] relates a story that occurred during the second *Beit Hamikdash* at a time when the Greeks ruled the land of Israel. A certain Miriam bat Bilga, daughter of a family of Kohanim, had married a Greek captain, and when the Greeks entered the sanctuary, she went in with them.

Upon seeing the Altar, she became emotional, feeling the pain of her people,[8] yet in her anger acted improperly and smacked her sandal on it, saying, "Wolf, wolf! For how long will you consume the wealth of Israel (who brought offerings upon it) and not stand by them in a time of need?"

When the Sages heard about it, after the victory of the Chashmonaim, they fined the entire "watch" of Kohanim of which her family was a part. The Sages reasoned that what a child says in the marketplace, he or she learned from its parents.

The Talmud asks, however: For one family, they fined the entire "watch"? Yes, answers the Talmud, because of the principle, "The wicked do bad, and this affects his neighbor."

(The converse also applies, indeed all the more so: "If good and blessing accrues to the righteous, then good and blessing will accrue to his neighbor" since the measure of good is greater than the measure of its opposite.)

7. *Sukkah* 56b.

8. See *Likkutei Sichot*, vol. 19, p. 64.

55

שְׁמִירַת הָעֵינַיִם—לְהִמָּנַע מִמַּרְאוֹת לֹא רְצוּיִים

Being careful what one looks at

The gift of vision is too precious to waste on negative or harmful things. The eyes are the gateway to the soul. Sight is how we take things that are external to us and bring them into ourselves. Willingly gazing at spiritually harmful things can damage our inner essence. For this reason, the Torah warns us to be careful what we look at.

In order to maintain a well-balanced spiritual character, a person must be able to summon up from within himself at certain times assertive and proactive energy in order to "do good"—*asei tov*. Similarly, a person must also, with the same will and energy, "refrain from doing bad"—*sur me'ra*—by maintaining a vigilant hold on the inner drives that can propel a person in the direction of self-indulgence and negativity.

This latter ability is vital so that a person will not come to do anything that is considered against Hashem and His will (as is explained in section 30). This is "the beginning and the main part and root of the service of Hashem" and is referred to as *Yirat Hashem* or *Yirat Shamayim*—"fear of Hashem" or "fear of Heaven."[1]

Among the primary expressions of this "fear of Heaven" is avoidance, not just of actual transgression but also of seeing (or hearing) something forbidden[2] since the gaze leads to and brings about actual transgression, as our Sages said,[3] "The eyes see, and the heart desires...."

This is especially true since that which enters a person through the eyes goes very deep and affects his entire inner spiritual framework, from his brain to his heart, to his very soul.

(This fact is alluded to in the verse that says[4] *Atah hareita ladaat...*—"You have been shown to know"—by being shown (seeing) you know, and knowledge is one

1. See *Tanya*, ch. 41.
2. *Kuntres Ha'avodah* beginning ch. 2.
3. *Tanchuma* 15. See *Rashi's* comment on Numbers 15:39.
4. Deuteronomy 4:35.

of the ten dimensions of the soul[5]—seeing reaches into the soul.)

A vision of something, even when young, can stay with a person forever and, if harmful, can corrode every fiber of his spirit.

Therefore, the main bulwark and protection against spiritual danger is control of one's eyes, as is written,[6] "Do not follow after your hearts and after your eyes, after which you stray."

The Sages advise us to make a "fence around transgression" and guard our eyes from seeing inappropriate things (see the story concerning Rashi above in section 4) and certainly not to gaze at evil.

The Maggid of Mezritch said that before looking at something, we should ask ourselves, "Am I looking at this in service of ***yotzri*** (my Creator) or ***yitzri*** (my evil inclination)?"[7]

A person who is not careful about what he sees transgresses a biblical prohibition as the verse quoted earlier says, "Do not stray after your hearts and after your eyes" (besides bringing great spiritual damage upon himself).

---

5. See section 30, above. Also *Sefer Kitzur Halachot l'Avot u'Banim*, 2: *Birchot Hashachar*, fn. 17.

6. Numbers 15:39.

7. *Vetzivah Hakohen*, ch. 13, citing R. Zev of Zhitomir in the name of the Maggid of Mezritch. See also *Iggeret Hakodesh*, 24, beg.

56

שְׁתִיקָה—הִמָּנְעוּת מִדִּבּוּר מְיֻתָּר

Silence

The Torah advises us that, in general, silence is preferable to speech. Mastering the faculty of speech by knowing when it is proper to speak and when it is better not to, is one of life's most precious talents.

Speech is very powerful—Hashem created the world with speech. It should therefore be treated carefully as it can have great impact—positive as well as negative.

Thus, the Torah advises that, in general, one should increase in silence. Our Sages stated,[1] "Silence is a fence for wisdom." Also,[2] "Silence is good for the wise, even more so for the foolish."

In general, a person is best served by decreasing his speech, and the Mishnaic sage Shamai taught,[3] "Say little, but do much."

It has been said,[4] "G-d created man with two ears but only one mouth to teach us that one should minimize his speech."

The Talmud says,[5] "If a word is (worth) one *sela* (a coin common in Talmudic times), silence is (worth) two." Also, "I did not find anything better for the body than silence"[6] and "Whoever speaks too much brings about transgression."[6]

For this reason, many of the sins enumerated in the Yom Kippur confessional prayer revolve around speech. The beginning of *teshuvah* thus involves **mastering the faculty of speech**—knowing when it is proper to speak and when it is proper to keep quiet.[7]

---

1. *Avot* 3:13.
2. *Pesachim* 99a.
3. *Avot* 1:15.
4. *Orchot Tzaddikim, Shaar Hashetikah.*
5. *Megillah* 18a.
6. *Avot* ibid.
7. It has been explained that fish in an aquarium or small fish tank can teach us a valuable lesson. Before they were caught, they roamed in large bodies of water, but now they are confined to a small space, usually with other fish. Yet they never fight with each other. The reason for this is because they cannot talk.

57

טָהֳרַת הַדִּבּוּר

Purity of speech

Man is not called "the thinker" or "the doer," rather "the speaker." The ability to communicate is what defines us and sets us apart, above all other creations of G-d. Being able to communicate is at the heart of life. It is only fitting therefore that our speech should reflect wisdom and refinement and be used for constructive and, if possible, holy and inspiring matters.

How we speak defines who we are.

This is because the ability to communicate is from the soul. And it is for this reason that a human being is called *hamedaber*—"the speaker"—because this is the superiority Hashem imbued us with over all other creations—the gift of speech.[1] When the Torah says,[2] "And man became a **living soul**," the Targum translates this as "And man became a **speaking soul**." Thus, **speech (i.e., the ability to communicate) is life.**

Therefore, how we use it reflects who we are.[3]

For this reason, **a person should always speak with appropriate and refined language,**[4] gently and if possible about holy matters (as is written,[5] "And you will speak in them" (i.e., in matters of Torah) and not in empty words of no value). Certainly, we should not contaminate our mouths with disgraceful words (G-d forbid).

The Torah, which in general is careful never to use even one unnecessary extra letter, nevertheless intentionally uses extra words when describing something unclean so as to describe it in pure and refined terminology, rather than use shorter but less graceful language.[6]

The Talmud[7] recounts a story concerning two students

---

1. See *Rosh Hashanah 5659—Divine Speech* (Kehot, 2015), where the concept of speech, being connected in its source to the very essence of the soul, is explained.

2. Genesis 2:7.

3. King David said in Psalms (35:10): *Kol atzmotai tomarno*—"All my limbs—my entire being—will speak...," implying that the essence of the soul ("*atzmotai*") comes to expression through speech (*Likutei Dibburim* vol. 4, p. 792).

4. *Pesachim* 3a. See *Haggadah Shel Pesach im Likutei Taamim, Uminhagim*, p. 17, where the insight of R. Yosef Yitzchak on the words: *Chacham mah hu omer*—literally—"What does the wise son say?" is elucidated with a change of punctuation to read: "*Chacham mah Hu?—Omer.*" "What is the wise one?—What he says."

5. Deuteronomy 6:7. (See *Yoma* 19b.)

6. *Pesachim* 3a.

7. Ibid. 3b.

of Hillel that illustrates the importance of refined language. Both posed the same question; however, one used refined terminology; while the other used less refined terms. Noting this Hillel said that the first student will become a great teacher of Torah in Israel. This student turned out to become the famous leader and Torah giant R. Yochanan ben Zakai.

Speech is called a "double-edged sword"[8]—it can lift man up and make him G-dly, or it can show his worst side. Therefore, we should habituate ourselves to think carefully before we speak (a word, like an arrow, once spoken cannot be brought back). Before speaking, one should consider not only whether what we wish to say is **true**, **necessary**, and **kind** (i.e., free of talebearing, gossip, and slander, and will not cause pain to another) but also if it is **appropriate** and **refined** language.

There is a second reason why it is so important to speak appropriately and with refinement, and that is because Hashem used speech to create everything and in this way gave us life through His speech, as the Mishnah says,[9] "With ten utterances was the world created," and as we say daily, *Baruch she'amar vehaya haolam*—"Blessed is the One Who **spoke** and the world came into being."

Hashem continues to do so, sustaining the world by means of His speech, as we say in the continuation of the above prayer, "Blessed is the One Who **speaks** and **makes** the world"—in the present tense.

This means that at this very moment, He creates the world just as He did at the first moment of creation, as we say in prayer, "Who renews in his goodness every day, constantly, the work of creation." All of this is

8. As alluded to in the words of Psalms 149:6.

9. *Avot* 5:1.

through speech, as was taught by the Baal Shem Tov on the verse:[10] "Forever, G-d, your word stands firm in Heaven," meaning to say that it is the word of G-d, Hashem's speech, that gives life to the Heavens, and indeed every created thing, constantly.[11]

A person who is sensitive to this and does not take G-d's constant gift of life for granted will therefore also try to speak in a way that is creative and not destructive, positive and not negative, refined and not coarse. **For surely, there is no greater display of ingratitude and effrontery to G-d than someone who uses his speech in a negative and destructive way, while G-d is using His speech to create and give life to that person.**

A third reason why it is so necessary to speak with refinement is because we use speech to connect to Hashem through prayer. It is only fitting that the vessel we use to ask Hashem for our needs should be pure.

Since the destruction of the Temple, the "offering of our lips," man's speech, in the form of our prayers, has taken the place of the sacrifices upon the Altar.

Just as a sacrifice was unacceptable if there was any impurity in it, so too our verbal sacrifice to G-d, our prayer, cannot properly be offered if the instruments of sacrifice, the mouth and the lips, are impure. **How can the same lips that speak improperly be used as a vehicle for sacrifice through prayer?**[12]

---

10. Psalms 119:89.

11. As explained in *Shaar Hayichud VehaEmunah*, ch. 1.

12. *Peleh Yoetz*: *Dibbur*. See *Shabbat* 33a: "Whoever uses impure speech, even if the Heavenly Court had sealed a favorable decree of seventy years for him, it will be reversed."

58

שֵׁם שָׁמַיִם שָׁגוּר בְּפִיךָ—
לְהַזְכִּיר אֶת שֵׁם ה' תָּמִיד

To constantly mention the Name of Heaven (G-d)

Expressing our constant connection to Hashem by mentioning Him in conversation reinforces our awareness of Him and brings home to us the fact that we are in His Presence at all times.

One of the ways in which we express our constant connection to Hashem and the fact that we are in His presence at all times is by mentioning Him habitually in our conversation. [1]

We learn this from Joseph, about whom it is written:[2] "His master saw that Hashem was with him," and *Rashi* explains that "Hashem was with him" means that "the name of Heaven was habitually in his mouth."

The story is told of the Baal Shem Tov,[3] that in the days before his revelation, he would travel from village to village and would ask Jewish men and women, young and old, about their situation, their health, wealth, and so on.

When they would answer with various phrases expressing praise and thanks to Hashem, such as "Thank G-d," or "May Hashem be praised," the Baal Shem Tov would be filled with joy.

Once, the Baal Shem Tov came to a certain place and, as was his holy way, gave the Jewish people the opportunity to praise Hashem. In that town, there lived an elderly Jew, learned in Torah, who practiced the ways of asceticism, studying and praying in the house of study all day and night.

When the Baal Shem Tov approached him asking about his health and whether he had what he needed,

---

1. One should not mention the name of Hashem directly, rather calling Him by a secondary descriptor, such as "Hashem" (and, in fact, we are careful not to mention the name of Hashem even in other languages, such as "G-d," and instead say "the Creator" or "the One above" and the like.)

2. Genesis 39:3.

3. *Sefer Hamaamarim—Yiddish*, p. 138. See also *Likkutei Sichot*, vol. 7, p. 135.

the old man did not answer or even look at the Baal Shem Tov.

The Baal Shem Tov continued to ask until the man became irritated and motioned that he should leave. The Baal Shem Tov asked: "Why will you not give Hashem His sustenance?" This made an impact on the man, who was puzzled; before him stood a seemingly simple Jew who spoke of the need to "give Hashem His sustenance"?!

The Baal Shem Tov sensed the thoughts of the man and said, "The Jews live off of the sustenance Hashem gives them. On what sustenance does Hashem live? King David said in Psalms:[4] 'You, Who are Holy, dwell on the praises of Israel.' Hashem is sustained by the praise and thanks of the Jewish people that they give Him in return for their health and wealth! And it is for these praises that Hashem gives Jews children, health, and wealth."

In this spirit, it is customary to thank Hashem by saying *Baruch Hashem* in conversation or when writing a letter, to begin with "ב"ה" or "בס"ד," being the initials of the phrase "Blessed be Hashem" or "With the help of Heaven."

Furthermore, a person should not say, "I will do such and such a thing," but rather, "I will do such and such a thing, *im yirtzeh Hashem*—if Hashem wills it" since "Many thoughts are in the heart of man,"[5] but not all of them will come to fruition; however, "the advice of Hashem, **it** will stand," [5] and the Hebrew initials of **it**

4. Psalms 22:4.

5. Proverbs 19:21.

(ה'י'א') are the same as those of the words אם ירצה ה'—"if Hashem wills it."

59

צַעַר בַּעֲלֵי חַיִּים"—הָאִסּוּר לְצַעֵר בַּעֲלֵי חַיִּים וְלִפְגּוֹעַ בָּהֶם"

The prohibition against causing harm to animals

One of the principles of our belief is that "Hashem is merciful to all His creatures." It is only fitting therefore for man to exhibit the same trait of kindness to animals and avoid cruelty to them, which the Torah forbids. Even more so by extension does this apply to people, for whom one must have the greatest kindness and care so as not to cause them pain or harm.

"G-d is good to all things, and his mercy is upon all of His works."[1] We, who imitate G-d and go in His ways, are commanded likewise to show compassion to animals and not cause them needless suffering or pain.[2]

Also, we must help them when they are in pain in order to reduce their suffering (as the verse says,[3] "When you see a donkey...crouching under its load...you will surely help it"). For example, if one sees an animal that has fallen under a heavy load, one must remove that load.[4]

Even one who eats before he feeds his animal (and all the more so if the animal stands and watches him eat) transgresses the prohibition against cruelty to animals, as we learn[5] from the order of the words in the verse: first it says[6] "And I gave grass in the field for your animals" and only afterward "And you will eat." Animals eat first since they depend on us as we depend on the Creator of the world; therefore, we must have mercy on them.

We are taught[7] that two of the greatest leaders of the Jewish people—Moses and David—were chosen to become the "shepherds" of G-d's people because of the compassion and special sensitivity they showed to each and every sheep they cared for as shepherds.

---

1. Psalms 145:9.

2. *Shabbat* 128b. *Rashi* there, caption: *Tza'ar Ba'alei Chaim. Bava Metzia* 32b. *Rambam, Hilchot Rotze'ach* 13:13. See *Shulchan Aruch Harav* 305:26: *Tza'ar baalei chaim* is a *mitzvah* of the Torah.

3. Exodus 23:5.

4. The Talmud (*Bava Metzia* 32b) says that since an animal already carrying a burden is in more pain than an animal being loaded, the *mitzvah* to help unload an animal takes precedence over the *mitzvah* to help load an animal, which is itself a specific mitzvah and is of help to the animal. See *Rambam, Hilchot Rotze'ach* 13: 1-4 and 13.

5. *Berachot* 40a.

6. Deuteronomy 11:15.

7. *Shemot Rabbah* 2:2.

Our Sages said:[8] "Whoever has mercy on the creations is treated mercifully by Heaven; that is, by the way man measures, so is he measured."[9]

In this vein, a story is told in the Talmud[10] concerning the great Sage, R. Yehudah Hanassi, compiler of the Mishnah.

Once, a calf was being brought to the slaughterhouse, and it ran and hid its head in the folds of R. Yehudah's clothes, crying that it did not want to be slaughtered. R. Yehudah said to the calf: "Go! For this you were created."

At that moment, it was said in Heaven, "Since he was not merciful toward the creations, Heaven's protective mercy will be removed from him and, he will endure suffering." And indeed, R. Yehudah endured suffering (stomach pains) for thirteen years.

One day, the maid was sweeping R. Yehudah's house and noticed weasels on the floor. She was about to sweep them out when R. Yehudah said, "Let them be since it is written,[1] 'His mercy is upon all of his works,' and therefore, we should be merciful even to weasels and not throw them out."

At that moment, it was said in Heaven, "Since he is merciful to the creations, we will be kind to him, and the suffering will therefore cease."

We see therefore that the Torah's compassion for animals is a trait that should be intrinsic to Jewish character.

---

8. *Shabbat* 151b.

9. *Megillah* 12b and other sources.

10. *Bava Metzia* 85a.

This is also reflected in the Torah's prohibition against combining milk and meat—whether eating, benefiting from, or cooking the two together. The latter uniquely reflects the extent to which the Torah negates harming animals and educates us in the trait of compassion.[11]

It is explained[12] that the prohibition of mixing milk with meat is forbidden also because of its cruelty to animals[13] since the foundation of that *mitzvah* is the ban on cooking a goat in its mother's milk, which is a great cruelty to the mother—milking her in order to cook her offspring in her own milk.

One of the lessons[14] that we can learn from this law is that if this is the case with animals, then all the more so regarding human beings—the utmost care should be taken not to cause any pain or harm (G-d forbid) to another person.

11. *Ramban*, Deuteronomy 14:21.

12. See *Likkutei Sichot* vol. 6, pp. 150-151, fn. 41.

13. *Likkutei Sichot* ibid.

14. *Likkutei Sichot* ibid, p. 151.

60

צִפִּיָּה לִגְאֻלָּה

The imperative of awaiting the coming of the Redemption and the revelation of *Mashiach*

Hope for, and belief in, the redemption is a cardinal principle of our faith. As Jews, we are aware of the imperfect state of the world. We long for the elevation and redemption of the world from its current state, where G-dliness is in "exile," to a time of perfection and revelation of G-dliness, which will be for the good of all mankind.

Faith in the coming of *Mashiach* and expectantly awaiting our salvation are among the foundations of the Jewish faith and religion.

Rambam writes:[1] "The King *Mashiach* will rise up and reinstate the ancient Kingship of David...and build the *Beit Hamikdash* and gather the exiles of the Jewish people...and whoever does not believe in him or who does not await his coming...denies the whole Torah. For the Torah itself speaks about him, as is stated:[2] And Hashem your G-d will bring back your exiles...even if you are spread out to the ends of Heaven...Hashem will bring you back."

Therefore, we should constantly desire and await this true and complete redemption and the building of the third *Beit Hamikdash* by our righteous *Mashiach*, may he come speedily in our days.[3]

In this way, **belief in the coming of *Mashiach* is a cardinal principle of our faith**[4] (in fact, the Talmud declares[5] that one of the first questions a person will be asked upon leaving this world will be: "Did you anticipate the redemption?").

The inner rationale that lies behind the centrality of this belief is because the advent of *Mashiach* is the purpose and end goal of the entire creation—all of the spiritual worlds and our physical world. It was all created in order that Hashem should have "a dwelling place in the lower

---

1. *Rambam, Hilchot Melachim* 11:1.

2. Deuteronomy 30:3-5.

3. *Rambam* ibid. Belief in *Mashiach* was included by the *Rambam* as one of the thirteen basic principles of our faith, where the concept is expressed with these words: "...I await him each day that he should come."

4. *Rambam* ibid. See *Likkutei Sichot* vol. 2, p. 599 and other numerous sources in *Likkutei Sichot*.

5. *Shabbat* 31a.

worlds," which will come to fruition with the advent of the Messianic Era.

The mission of the Jewish people, since the founding of our People, has been with the end purpose of **changing the nature of creation to make it a "dwelling place for the Divine Presence in this world." This is the grandest enterprise of all time. It is a vast collaborative effort involving every person, every life span, and every action, whether it be direct or indirect, commencing with creation and culminating with the advent of *Mashiach*, all working together to change the nature of creation from an environment innately hostile to the revelation of G-dliness to one open and naturally receptive of revealed G-dliness.**

This change will come to fruition through the service of Torah and *mitzvot* during our time in exile, using physical things for *mitzvot* (which are the will of Hashem) and in this way transforming the physical into a vessel for G-dliness, thus "refining pure from the impure."

When this refinement brings the world to its culminating perfection as a vessel for G-dliness—a dwelling place for Hashem in this world, with the coming of the ultimate redemption—then the work of all the generations of Jews will be complete. The G-dliness hidden within our material existence will be revealed to all through the drawing down of Hashem's presence, the *Shechinah* ("and not only His presence but the main part of His presence"[6]), into the lower worlds.

In this way, will the "good be refined from the bad," in the sense that the Jewish people will leave their

6. *Torat Menachem—Sefer Hamaamarim Bati Legani*, vol. 1, p. 7.

exile among the other nations of the world, and this will bring the entire world to serve Hashem together, for the entire world will be full of Hashem's revealed Kingship, forever.

In this state, with the return of the kingship to the house of David, the rebuilding of our *Beit Hamikdash*, and the ingathering of the exiles through *Mashiach*, it will be possible once again to fulfill the *mitzvot* of G-d's Torah to perfection—all this culminating in the era of the resurrection.[7]

Therefore,[8] "yearning and looking forward to salvation" and the faith that this will one day be a reality, may this be speedily in our days, is a cardinal principle in Judaism and is a belief that our fathers lived with throughout the ages.

The Lubavitcher Rebbe emphasized the extent to which **we should not accept nor be satisfied with our state of "exile," being the state in which Hashem's presence in creation is concealed** and in which we, His people, are like[9] "children banished from their father's table," who have not yet been welcomed back.

Since we were exiled against our will—it was our Father who banished us from our Land and sent us into the

THE BATTLE

Many may think: "What does it matter that one day *Mashiach* will arrive? I just need to do what I am commanded to do and keep Hashem's *mitzvot*. It's not for me to know what the purpose of my service is and its end result." However, this is a mistaken approach. An analogy is given of the soldier who is not told "why" he is fighting and therefore will only do as much as he is commanded and no more, which may weaken the war effort, compared to the soldier who knows the purpose of the war, why he is fighting, and the great prize awaiting a victorious outcome. Such a soldier will fight with far higher morale, greater

---

7. See *Rambam, Pirush Hamishnayot Sanhedrin, Chapter: Kol Yisrael—The Thirteen Principles of Faith*. See *Likkutei Sichot* vol. 27, p. 198.

8. See *Likkutei Sichot*, vol. 28, p. 135. See also *Shiurim b'Torat Chabad* (R. Yoel Kahn), chapter entitled *Geulah*, where the centrality to Torah and *mitzvot* of belief in Mashiach is explained.

9. *Berachot* 3a.

exile—we therefore have the ability to withstand all of its travails and remain faithful to His service, yet feeling all along the great lacking and pain of exile.[10]

Furthermore, the Rebbe stressed with great emphasis the importance of looking forward to salvation with the faith that "the time of your redemption has come," may it occur speedily and in our days. He stressed many times that every individual has the ability, and even more so, the obligation to bring the redemption closer and to bring about the revelation of *Mashiach* (by increasing observance of Torah and *mitzvot*), which will transform this world into G-d's ultimate home.

spirit, and more ingenuity, doing all in his power to win the war. So, too, every Jew should know that serving Hashem is part of the war between the side of holiness—"*kedushah*," which exists to bring holiness into this world and in this way create "a dwelling place for Hashem in this world," and the side of unholiness—"*kelipah*," which is fighting to prevent that. Every mitzvah we do brings G-dliness (the *Shechinah*) down into the world, thus creating a dwelling place for Hashem here and in this way bringing about the future revelation of G-dliness in the world with the revelation of *Mashiach*. This is the entire purpose of creation, and for this reason, belief in the future redemption through *Mashiach* is fundamental to our faith.

10. See *Likkutei Sichot*, vol. 30, p. 235.

Index

A

Aaron, 229n2
ability, Hashem's requests according to, 37-40
Achav, 173
achilah, 156
Achimelech, 172n2
acknowledging goodness, 58-62
acting in a seemingly sinful way, not, 189-191
actions being for the sake of Heaven, all, 45-47
Adam, 76n3, 158n3, 164
Adon Olam, 13
Agrippa, King, 207-208
ahavat chinam, 139
ahavat Yisrael. *See* love for a fellow Jew
akeidah, 71, 74n10
Akiva, R.
  blessing Hashem for both positive and negative, 24
  emulation of Hashem through charity, 149
  judging everyone favorably, 168
  love for a fellow Jew, 135
  overcoming desire for retribution, 99
  persistence, 84
  seeing every situation as good, 20-22
  visiting the sick, 158-159
Al Hanissim, 61
alacrity in service of Hashem, 70-74
alef-bet, 85, 89
Aleinu, 66
Alexandri, R., 174
Altar, 146, 155, 240
Alter Rebbe
  all actions being for the sake of Heaven, 46
  belief in Hashem, 4
  emulation of Hashem through charity, 146n10, 147, 152
  energy, enthusiasm, and alacrity in service of Hashem, 71
  generosity of spirit and giving way to others, 106
  Hashem's requests according to ability, 39
  head ruling over heart, 78
  keeping away from anger, 101
  love for a fellow Jew, 137
  recognizing one's own qualities, 114
  rejoicing in one's lot, 68n2
  serving Hashem with joy, 51n2, 54n8
Amidah, 60
anger, keeping away from, 100-104

animals, prohibition against harming, 245-248
another, not embarrassing, 185-188
another, not seeing negative in, 178-180
another, prohibition against causing pain to, 202-205
another, prohibition against striking, 212-214
another's feelings, prohibition against hurting, 202-205
another's possessions, prohibition against desiring, 199-201
another's property, prohibition against damaging, 210-211
appreciating the value of time, 119-122
Arizal, 56, 103-104
Asher Yatzar, 130
Ashrei, 88
association with righteous people, necessity of, 228-231
avak lashon hara, 175-176
aveirah goreret aveirah, 125
Avishai ben Tzruyah, 102
avodat Hashem, 10, 16, 71, 73, 87n4, 152, 251
avoiding danger, 222-224
avoiding spiritual danger, 123-126
Avraham
- appreciating the value of time, 120n2
- comforting those in mourning, 161
- emulation of Hashem through charity, 145
- energy, enthusiasm, and alacrity in service of Hashem, 71, 74n10
- generosity of spirit and giving way to others, 107-108
- the *mitzvah* of hospitality, 154, 156
- satisfaction even with little, 65
- seeing every situation as good, 21
- visiting the sick, 158

Avshalom, 102
awaiting the coming of the Redemption and the revelation of Mashiach, 249-253

B

Ba'al Shem Tov
- belief in Divine Providence, 12, 13n7
- belief in Hashem, 3
- blessing Hashem for both positive and negative, 25
- constantly mentioning the name of Hashem, 242-243
- emulation of Hashem through charity, 144
- energy, enthusiasm, and alacrity in service of Hashem, 73n9
- humility and self-effacement, 112
- judging everyone favorably, 166-167
- learning life lessons from everything, 15-18
- love for a fellow Jew, 136, 138, 140
- mindfulness of Hashem, 8, 10

not being wasteful, 227
not seeing negative in another, 179
persistence, 84n1
prohibition against talebearing, gossip, and slander, 176
purity of speech, 240
serving Hashem with joy, 52
trust in Hashem, 30n8
truthfulness, 90n15, 91
ba'alei teshuvah, 115n4
bal tashchit. *See* not being wasteful
Baruch She'amar, 239
being careful of what one looks at, 232-234
being idle while blood being spilled, not, 163-164
being wasteful, not, 225-227
Beit Hamikdash
awaiting the coming of the Redemption and the revelation of Mashiach, 250, 252
emulation of Hashem through charity, 146
gratitude and acknowledging goodness, 59
judging everyone favorably, 169
living over obstacles, 80–81
love for a fellow Jew, 138
the *mitzvah* of hospitality, 155
necessity to associate with righteous people, 231
never quarreling over a *mitzvah*, 142
not acting in a seemingly sinful way, 190
prohibition against false flattery, 207-208
purity of speech, 240
belief in Divine Providence, 11-14
belief in Hashem, 2-6
bikkurim, 59-60
bitachon, 27-31, 33
bitul, 107n4, 111
blessing Hashem for both positive and negative, 23-26
blind, not placing an obstacle before the, 215-217
blood being spilled, not being idle while, 163-164

C

careful of what one looks at, being, 232-234
causing pain to another, prohibition against, 202-205
chanifah, 207
Channah, 42n2
Chanukah, 66
charity, 140, 143-152, 159
Chashmonaim, 231
Chava, 158n3
cheating, prohibition against, 202-205
chesaron, 125
chesed, 25n6, 107, 146, 154, 158, 161-162
Chevra Kadisha, 162
chillul Hashem, 43, 207, 219
chochmah, 103
comforting those in mourning, 160-162
coming of the Redemption, awaiting the, 249-253

constantly mentioning the name of Hashem, 241-244

D

damaging another's property, prohibition against, 210-211
dan l'kaf zechut. *See* judging everyone favorably
danger, avoiding, 222-224
danger, avoiding spiritual, 123-126
David, King
- avoiding spiritual danger, 124, 126
- awaiting the coming of the Redemption and the revelation of Mashiach, 250, 252
- blessing Hashem for both positive and negative, 25n6
- constantly mentioning the name of Hashem, 243
- gratitude and acknowledging goodness, 59, 61-62
- keeping away from anger, 101-102
- measure for measure, 36
- mindfulness of Hashem, 8
- never losing hope, 34
- prohibition against harming animals, 246
- prohibition against talebearing, gossip, and slander, 172n2, 173
- purity of speech, 238n3
- serving Hashem with joy, 51
- trust in Hashem, 30-31
- truthfulness, 91

Dayeinu, 61n7
deceit, prohibition against verbal, 202-205
deception, prohibition against, 196-198
desecration of Hashem's name. *See chillul Hashem*
desire for retribution, overcoming, 98-99
desiring another's possessions, prohibition against, 199-201
Divine Presence. *See Shechinah*
Divine Providence, 10-14, 18, 20, 30-31, 53, 179
Doeg, 172n2

E

Egypt, 59, 111n9
Egyptians, 36n4
Eitz Yosef, 88n9
Elazar, R., 147
Elazar ben Durdia, R., 72
Eliezer, R., 99, 107
Eliezer ben Horkanus, R., 168
Elijah the Prophet, 21
embarrassing another, not, 185-188
emulation of Hashem through charity, 143-152
emunah, 2-6, 8, 27-28, 93
energy in service of Hashem, 70-74
enthusiasm in service of Hashem, 70-74
ephod, 16-17
Eve. *See* Chava
evil inclination. *See yetzer hara*
Exodus, 61n7
Ezrat Avotainu, 183

F

false flattery, prohibition against, 206-209
favorably, judging everyone, 165-170
feelings, prohibition against hurting another's, 202-205
fellow Jew, love for a, 134-140
flattery, prohibition against false, 206-209
fulfilling personal resolutions, 95-97
Futerfas, R. Mendel, 5-6, 9-10, 74, 90

G

ga'avah, 114n2
G-d. *See* Hashem
gematria, 158n3
gemilut chasadim. *See chesed*
generosity of spirit, 105-108
Gentiles. *See* non-Jews
giving way to others, 105-108
g'neivah, 193
g'neivat da'at, 197
good, seeing every situation as, 19-22
goodness, acknowledging, 58-62
gossip, prohibition against, 171-177
gratitude, 58-62
Greeks, 231
grudge, not holding a, 181-184
guarding one's health, 127-131
guide, need for a life, 116-118
g'zeilah, 193

H

Habakkuk, 5n10
hachnasat orchim. *See* hospitality, the *mitzvah* of
hakarat hatov. *See* gratitude
Hakhel, 208
halbanat pnei chavero. *See* not embarrassing another
Hallel, 61
harming animals, prohibition against, 245-248
Hashem
    all actions being for the sake of Heaven, 45-46
    appreciating the value of time, 120-121
    avoiding danger, 222-223
    avoiding spiritual danger, 124-125
    awaiting the coming of the Redemption and the revelation of Mashiach, 249-253
    being careful of what one looks at, 233
    belief in, 2-6
    belief in Divine Providence, 11-14
    blessing for both positive and negative, 23-26
    comforting those in mourning, 160-162
    constantly mentioning the name of, 241-244
    emulation of through charity, 143-152
    energy, enthusiasm, and alacrity in service of, 70-74
    fulfilling personal resolutions, 95-96

generosity of spirit and giving way to others, 106-107
gratitude and acknowledging goodness, 58-62
guarding one's health, 127-128
head ruling over heart, 76-77, 78n9
humility and self-effacement, 109-112
joy derived from *mitzvot*, 55-56
judging everyone favorably, 165, 167-170
keeping away from anger, 100-103
learning life lessons from everything, 15-18
living over obstacles, 80-82
love for a fellow Jew, 134, 136-138, 140
measure for measure, 36
mindfulness of, 7-10
the *mitzvah* of hospitality, 153-154
need for a life guide and mentor, 117-118
never losing hope, 33-34
never quarreling over a *mitzvah*, 142
not acting in a seemingly sinful way, 189-191
not being idle while blood being spilled, 164
not being wasteful, 225, 227
not embarrassing another, 186
not seeing negative in another, 178, 180
not taking revenge or holding a grudge, 181, 183-184
our relationship with, 1-47
overcoming desire for retribution, 99
persistence, 84-85
prohibition against causing pain to another, 203-204
prohibition against deception, 198
prohibition against desiring another's possessions, 199-201
prohibition against false flattery, 207
prohibition against harming animals, 245-246
prohibition against striking another, 212-213
prohibition against talebearing, gossip, and slander, 171, 174
prohibition against theft and robbery, 192-195
purity of speech, 237-240
recognizing one's own qualities, 114-115
rejoicing in one's lot, 67-69
requests of according to ability, 37-40
requirement to return lost objects, 219-220
sanctification of the name of, 41-44
satisfaction even with little, 63-64, 66
seeing every situation as good, 19-22
serving with joy, 50-54
trust in, 27-31
trustworthiness, 92
truthfulness, 86-91

virtue of silence, 236
visiting the sick, 157-158
hashgachah pratit. *See* Divine Providence
Hatarat Nedarim, 94n6
hatmadah, 84
head ruling over heart, 75-78
health, guarding one's, 127-131
heart, head ruling over, 75-78
Heaven, all actions being for the sake of, 45-47
Herod, King, 207
Hezekiah, King, 33-34, 62, 82n2
Hillel, 129n5, 135-137, 239
hin, 93
hishtavut, 25
holding a grudge, not, 181-184
hope, never losing, 32-34
Horkanus, 169
hospitality, the *mitzvah* of, 153-156
humility, 109-112
hurting another's feelings, prohibition against, 202-205

I

idle, not being while blood being spilled, 163-164
Isaiah, 31, 33-34
Ishmaelites, 43-44
Israel, Land of, 38n1, 173, 226

J

Jerusalem, 80-81
Jew, love for a fellow, 134-140
Joshua, 82
joy
blessing for both positive and negative, 24-25
constantly mentioning the name of Hashem, 242
derived from *mitzvot*, 55-57
emulation of Hashem through charity, 146, 148-149
energy, enthusiasm, and alacrity in service of Hashem, 71, 74n10
generosity of spirit and giving way to others, 106
guarding one's health, 131
Hashem's requests according to ability, 39
humility and self-effacement, 110
love for a fellow Jew, 135
mindfulness of Hashem, 9n4
not embarrassing another, 187
rejoicing in one's lot, 67-69
sanctification of Hashem's name, 43
satisfaction even with little, 64
serving Hashem with, 50-54
trust in Hashem, 29
judging everyone favorably, 165-170

K

Kabbalah, 136
kabolat ol, 124
kashrut, 216, 248
kedushah, 253
keeping away from anger, 100-104
kelipot, 76n4, 107n4, 253
kiddush Hashem. *See* sanctification of Hashem's name
Kitzur Shulchan Aruch, 128
Kletzker, R. Binyamin, 4

Kohanim, 190, 231
Kol Nidrei, 94
Korach, 230

L

lashon hara, 172-176, 179
lashon tov, 176
learning life lessons from everything, 15-18
Leningrad, 5
lessons of life, learning from everything, 15-18
leviyah, 155-156
life guide and mentor, need for a, 116-118
life lessons, learning from everything, 15-18
lifnei iveir. *See* not placing an obstacle before the blind
little, satisfaction even with, 63-66
living over obstacles, 79-82
looking at, being careful of what one is, 232-234
losing hope, never, 32-34
lost objects, requirement to return, 218-220
lot, rejoicing in one's, 67-69
love for a fellow Jew, 134-140, 158, 161, 183, 217, 220
l'toelet, lashon hara, 175

M

ma'aser, 169
ma'avir al midotav, 99, 182
machloket, 142n1
Maggid of Mezritch, 24, 128, 234
Maharash, Rebbe, 12n3, 80
Maimonides. *See* Rambam
Mar Ukva, 187
marit ayin, 190
Mashiach, 62, 249-253
mashpia, 117
measure for measure, 27, 29, 35-36, 99, 147, 208
Meisels, R. Moshe, 78
Menachem Mendel, R. *See* Tzemach Tzedek
menorah, 66
mentioning the name of Hashem, constantly, 241-244
mentor, need for a life, 116-118
mesirat nefesh, 78n9
Messianic Era, 251
middot, 106, 182n4
Midrash, 59-60, 68n3
mindfulness of Hashem, 7-10
Miriam bat Bilga, 231
Mishnah, 51, 72, 166-167, 239, 247
Mitteler Rebbe, 117
mitzvah goreret mitzvah, 125
mitzvot
- appreciating the value of time, 121
- avoiding spiritual danger, 125-126n8
- awaiting the coming of the Redemption and the revelation of Mashiach, 251-253
- belief in Hashem, 2, 3n1, 5
- comforting those in mourning, 161-162
- emulation of Hashem through charity, 144-146, 150, 152
- energy, enthusiasm, and

alacrity in service of Hashem, 71-73, 74n10
generosity of spirit and giving way to others, 107
gratitude and acknowledging goodness, 59
guarding one's health, 128
Hashem's requests according to ability, 38-39
head ruling over heart, 78n9
hospitality, 153-156
joy derived from, 55-57
judging everyone favorably, 166
keeping away from anger, 104
learning life lessons from everything, 17
living over obstacles, 81
love for a fellow Jew, 135-138, 140
mindfulness of Hashem, 8-9
necessity to associate with righteous people, 230
never quarreling over, 141-142
not being idle while blood being spilled, 164
not being wasteful, 226
not placing an obstacle before the blind, 216
prohibition against false flattery, 208
prohibition against harming animals, 246n4, 248
prohibition against striking another, 213
prohibition against talebearing, gossip, and slander, 173
requirement to return lost objects, 220
sanctification of Hashem's name, 41
satisfaction even with little, 66
serving Hashem with joy, 51
truthfulness, 90-91
visiting the sick, 158-159

Modeh Ani, 6
Modim, 60
Moshc
belief in Hashem, 4-6
comforting those in mourning, 162
emulation of Hashem through charity, 145
gratitude and acknowledging goodness, 59
humility and self-effacement, 111, 111n9
living over obstacles, 82
necessity to associate with righteous people, 229n2, 230
prohibition against false flattery, 209n8
prohibition against harming animals, 246
recognizing one's own qualities, 114
visiting the sick, 158n3

motzei shem ra, 175
motzui rishon, 3n1
mourning, comforting those in, 160-162
Munbaz, King, 148

N

Nachshon, 39n6
Nachum Ish Gamzu, 21-22
Nakdimon ben Gurion, 80-82

name, sanctification of Hashem's, 41-44
name of Hashem, constantly mentioning the, 241-244
Napoleon, 78
necessity to associate with righteous people, 228-231
Nechunia ben Hakanah, R., 106
need for a life guide and mentor, 116-118
negative, blessing Hashem for both positive and, 23-26
negative in another, not seeing, 178-180
neshamah
avoiding danger, 223
avoiding spiritual danger, 124
being careful of what one looks at, 232-234
belief in Hashem, 5-6
comforting those in mourning, 160-162
emulation of Hashem through charity, 151-152
energy, enthusiasm, and alacrity in service of Hashem, 72
generosity of spirit and giving way to others, 105, 108
gratitude and acknowledging goodness, 59
guarding one's health, 128, 129n5, 131
Hashem's requests according to ability, 39
judging everyone favorably, 168
keeping away from anger, 103
love for a fellow Jew, 134, 136-137, 140
mindfulness of Hashem, 8
necessity to associate with righteous people, 230
need for a life guide and mentor, 117-118
never quarreling over a *mitzvah*, 142n1
not being idle while blood being spilled, 164
not being wasteful, 226
persistence, 84n1
prohibition against theft and robbery, 193n2
purity of speech, 238
recognizing one's own qualities, 113-114, 115n4
requirement to return lost objects, 220
sanctification of Hashem's name, 42
satisfaction even with little, 65
serving Hashem with joy, 51n2, 53
trust in Hashem, 30
visiting the sick, 158-159
never losing hope, 32-34
never quarreling over a *mitzvah*, 141-142
Nile River, 59
Nishmat Kol Chai, 61
Nob, 172n2
non-Jews, 18, 43, 207-208, 219
not acting in a seemingly sinful way, 189-191
not being idle while blood being spilled, 163-164

not being wasteful, 225-227
not embarrassing another, 185-188
not holding a grudge, 181-184
not placing an obstacle before the blind, 215-217
not seeing negative in another, 178-180
not taking revenge, 181-184

O

objects, requirement to return lost, 218-220
obstacle before the blind, not placing an, 215-217
obstacles, living over, 79-82
ona'at devarim, 175, 203, 205
others, giving way to, 105-108
others, our relationship with, 133-220
Otzar Hat'fillot, 88n9
ourselves, our relationship with, 49-131
overcoming desire for retribution, 98-99
own qualities, recognizing one's, 113-115

P

pain to another, prohibition against causing, 202-205
persistence, 83-85
personal resolutions, fulfilling, 95-97
Pesach, 61n7, 80
Pinchas, 39n6
Pirkei Avos, 117
placing an obstacle before the blind, not, 215-217
positive and negative, blessing Hashem for both, 23-26
possessions, prohibition against desiring another's, 199-201
prayer
- avoiding spiritual danger, 125
- belief in Divine Providence, 12-13
- belief in Hashem, 4-6
- constantly mentioning the name of Hashem, 242
- emulation of Hashem through charity, 147
- energy, enthusiasm, and alacrity in service of Hashem, 71
- fulfilling personal resolutions, 96
- generosity of spirit and giving way to others, 107
- gratitude and acknowledging goodness, 59-61
- judging everyone favorably, 167
- living over obstacles, 81-82
- love for a fellow Jew, 136
- never losing hope, 32, 34
- not taking revenge or holding a grudge, 183
- overcoming desire for retribution, 98-99
- purity of speech, 239-240
- satisfaction even with little, 66
- serving Hashem with joy, 52n6, 53
- trust in Hashem, 30n8
- trustworthiness, 94
- truthfulness, 87-88, 90
- virtue of silence, 236

visiting the sick, 159
prohibition against causing pain to another, 202-205
prohibition against damaging another's property, 210-211
prohibition against deception, 196-198
prohibition against desiring another's possessions, 199-201
prohibition against false flattery, 206-209
prohibition against harming animals, 245-248
prohibition against striking another, 212-214
prohibition against talebearing, gossip, and slander, 171-177
prohibition against theft and robbery, 192-195
property, prohibition against damaging another's, 210-211
Psalms
avoiding spiritual danger, 126n9
blessing Hashem for both positive and negative, 25
constantly mentioning the name of Hashem, 243
gratitude and acknowledging goodness, 59, 61
keeping away from anger, 101
measure for measure, 36
mindfulness of Hashem, 8
serving Hashem with joy, 51
trust in Hashem, 30
truthfulness, 87
purity of speech, 237-240

Q

qualities, recognizing one's own, 113-115
quarreling over a *mitzvah*, never, 141-142

R

Radak, 12n1, 88n9
Rambam
awaiting the coming of the Redemption and the revelation of Mashiach, 250
belief in Hashem, 3n1
comforting those in mourning, 161
generosity of spirit and giving way to others, 106n1
guarding one's health, 128, 130
love for a fellow Jew, 138
necessity to associate with righteous people, 229
not taking revenge or holding a grudge, 182n4
requirement to return lost objects, 219
visiting the sick, 158
Ran, 223n6
Rashab, Rebbe, 16n1, 124, 188n7
Rashi
being careful of what one looks at, 234
constantly mentioning the name of Hashem, 242
humility and self-effacement, 110n4
learning life lessons from everything, 16-17
measure for measure, 36n2

not taking revenge or holding a grudge, 183n8
prohibition against damaging another's property, 211n3
truthfulness, 89n11
Rayatz, Rebbe, 71n1, 211, 238n4
Rebbe, the
awaiting the coming of the Redemption and the revelation of Mashiach, 252-253
belief in Divine Providence, 13
belief in Hashem, 3n1, 4n7
emulation of Hashem through charity, 150
generosity of spirit and giving way to others, 107nn4-5
judging everyone favorably, 167n7
learning life lessons from everything, 16n1
love for a fellow Jew, 138, 140
need for a life guide and mentor, 117
recognizing one's own qualities, 115n4
trust in Hashem, 30n7
rechilut, 172, 175
recognizing one's own qualities, 113-115
Redemption, 33, 249-253
refuah shelaimah. See visiting the sick
Reishit Chachmah, 103n12
rejoicing in one's lot, 67-69
relationship with Hashem, our, 1-47
relationship with others, our, 133-220
relationship with ourselves, our, 49-131
relationship with the world, our, 221-253
requests according to ability, Hashem's, 37-40
requirement to return lost objects, 218-220
resolutions, fulfilling personal, 95-97
retribution, overcoming desire for, 98-99
returning lost objects, requirement of, 218-220
Reuven, 230
revelation of Mashiach, awaiting the, 249-253
revenge, not taking, 181-184
righteous people, necessity to associate with, 228-231
Rivkah, 107-108
robbery, prohibition against, 192-195
Romans, 21, 80-82
Rome, 21, 172
Rosh Chodesh, 5
Rosh Hashanah, 52, 71, 94n6, 194
Russia, 5, 78, 90

S

Safra, Rav, 96
sanctification of Hashem's name, 41-44, 191, 219
Satan, 223
satisfaction even with little, 63-66
Saul, King, 172n2

Seder, 61n7
seeing every situation as good, 19-22
seeing negative in another, not, 178-180
self-effacement, 109-112
service of Hashem, energy, enthusiasm, and alacrity in, 70-74
serving Hashem with joy, 50-54
Shabbat, 5
Shamai, 236
Shavuot, 80
Shechinah, 103, 157-158, 251, 253
Shema, 3-4, 78n9, 96
shidduchim, 68n3
Shimi ben Gaira, 102
Shimon ben Shetach, R., 43-44, 219
shlichut, 230
Shmuel, R. *See* Maharash, Rebbe
shtiyah, 156
Shulchan Aruch, 8-9, 72
Siberia, 5-6, 90-91
sick, visiting the, 157-159
silence, virtue of, 235-236
simchah. *See* joy
Sinai, Mount, 5-6, 8, 111n9
sinat chinam, 101, 138-139
sinful way, not acting in a seemingly, 189-191
sitra achara, 107n4
situation, seeing as good every, 19-22
slander, prohibition against, 171-177
Solomon, King, 9n4, 54, 104n15, 130
soul. *See neshamah*
Spalerno Prison, 5-6
speech, purity of, 237-240
spilled, not being idle while blood being, 163-164
spirit, generosity of, 105-108
spiritual danger, avoiding, 123-126
Stalin, Joseph, 6, 9
striking another, prohibition against, 212-214
Sukkot, 6, 80, 169
Suria, 172
s'yata di'shmayah, 46
synagogue, 142

T

taking revenge, not, 181-184
talebearing, prohibition against, 171-177
Talmud
  all actions being for the sake of Heaven, 46
  awaiting the coming of the Redemption and the revelation of Mashiach, 250
  emulation of Hashem through charity, 144, 147-149, 151
  fulfilling personal resolutions, 96
  generosity of spirit and giving way to others, 106
  guarding one's health, 131
  Hashem's requests according to ability, 38-39
  head ruling over heart, 78n9
  judging everyone favorably, 168
  keeping away from anger, 101, 103-104

living over obstacles, 80, 82
necessity to associate with righteous people, 230-231
need for a life guide and mentor, 117, 118n3
never losing hope, 33
not acting in a seemingly sinful way, 191
not being idle while blood being spilled, 164
not being wasteful, 226
not embarrassing another, 187-188
not taking revenge or holding a grudge, 182, 184
overcoming desire for retribution, 99
prohibition against causing pain to another, 204
prohibition against false flattery, 207-208
prohibition against harming animals, 246n4, 247
prohibition against talebearing, gossip, and slander, 172-174
prohibition against theft and robbery, 193-194
purity of speech, 238
recognizing one's own qualities, 115n4
rejoicing in one's lot, 69n3
requirement to return lost objects, 219
sanctification of Hashem's name, 43
seeing every situation as good, 20-21
trust in Hashem, 30n7
trustworthiness, 93
truthfulness, 87
virtue of silence, 236
visiting the sick, 158
Tanya, 4n10, 39, 54n8
Targum, 238
temimut, 198, 209
Temple. *See Beit Hamikdash*
Ten Commandments, 2-3, 5, 200-201
teshuvah, 36, 72, 101, 174, 236
theft, prohibition against, 192-195
Thirteen Principles of Faith, 250n3
time, appreciating the value of, 119-122
Torah
all actions being for the sake of Heaven, 45-46
appreciating the value of time, 120-122
avoiding danger, 222
avoiding spiritual danger, 124
awaiting the coming of the Redemption and the revelation of Mashiach, 250-253
being careful of what one looks at, 232
belief in Divine Providence, 12
comforting those in mourning, 161-162
constantly mentioning the name of Hashem, 242
emulation of Hashem through charity, 144, 147, 152
energy, enthusiasm, and alacrity in service of Hashem, 70, 73

generosity of spirit and giving way to others, 107
gratitude and acknowledging goodness, 59n1, 60
guarding one's health, 127-128, 130
head ruling over heart, 76, 78n9
humility and self-effacement, 111n9
judging everyone favorably, 166n3, 167-169
learning life lessons from everything, 16-17
love for a fellow Jew, 134-138, 140
mindfulness of Hashem, 8-9
necessity to associate with righteous people, 229-230
need for a life guide and mentor, 117
never losing hope, 34n5
not acting in a seemingly sinful way, 189
not being idle while blood being spilled, 163-164
not being wasteful, 225-227
not embarrassing another, 187
not placing an obstacle before the blind, 215-216
persistence, 84-85
prohibition against causing pain to another, 202-203
prohibition against damaging another's property, 210
prohibition against deception, 197
prohibition against desiring another's possessions, 200
prohibition against false flattery, 206-209
prohibition against harming animals, 245, 247-248
prohibition against striking another, 213
prohibition against talebearing, gossip, and slander, 171-173, 175
prohibition against theft and robbery, 194-195
purity of speech, 238-239
requirement to return lost objects, 218, 220
sanctification of Hashem's name, 41, 43
satisfaction even with little, 63-64, 66
serving Hashem with joy, 50-51, 52n6
trustworthiness, 93
truthfulness, 87-90
virtue of silence, 235-236
visiting the sick, 158

tov ayin, 135
trust in Hashem, 27-31
trustworthiness, 92-94
truthfulness, 86-91
tzaddikim, 114, 115n4
tzar ayin, 135
tzedakah. *See* charity
Tzemach Tzedek, 29, 54n8, 118n3, 140n14
tzniut, 112n12

V

value of time, appreciating the, 119-122

vatranut, 106
v'dover emet bilvavo, 96
verbal deceit, prohibition against, 202-205
Vidui, 236
virtue of silence, 235-236
visiting the sick, 157-159

W

wasteful, not being, 225-227
world, our relationship with the, 221-253
World to Come, 72, 115n4, 148-149, 158, 188
World War II, 5, 90

Y

Ya'akov, 65, 82n2
Yehudah, 230
Yehudah ben Teimah, 72
Yehudah HaNassi, R., 72, 247
yesh mei'ayin, 3n3
yetzer hara
  avoiding spiritual danger, 125
  being careful of what one looks at, 234
  energy, enthusiasm, and alacrity in service of Hashem, 72
  Hashem's requests according to ability, 38-39
  head ruling over heart, 76n5, 78n9
  love for a fellow Jew, 139
  never quarreling over a *mitzvah*, 142
  not placing an obstacle before the blind, 216n4
yirat Shamayim, 124, 233
Yishmael, 107n4
Yissachar, 230
Yitro, 36n4
Yitzchak, 65, 71, 74n10, 107, 161
yiush shelo mida'at, 34n4
Yochanan ben Zakai, R., 239
Yom Kippur, 5-6, 94, 168, 236
Yom Tov, 5
Yosef, 242
Yosei, R., 68n3

Z

zechut, 167n7
Zeira, R., 104
Zevulun, 230
Zohar, 54
z'rizut, 71-73
Zusha of Hanipol, R., 24-25, 88n8, 114